# U.S. YEARBOOK

ISBN: 9798323263547

*Cover: Canned beer goes on sale to the public for the first time in Richmond, Virginia.*

# INDEX

**FIRST EDITION**

### January

| S | M | T | W | T | F | S |
|---|---|---|---|---|---|---|
|   |   | 1 | 2 | 3 | 4 | 5 |
| 6 | 7 | 8 | 9 | 10 | 11 | 12 |
| 13 | 14 | 15 | 16 | 17 | 18 | 19 |
| 20 | 21 | 22 | 23 | 24 | 25 | 26 |
| 27 | 28 | 29 | 30 | 31 |   |   |

●:5  ◐:11  ○:19  ◑:27

### February

| S | M | T | W | T | F | S |
|---|---|---|---|---|---|---|
|   |   |   |   |   | 1 | 2 |
| 3 | 4 | 5 | 6 | 7 | 8 | 9 |
| 10 | 11 | 12 | 13 | 14 | 15 | 16 |
| 17 | 18 | 19 | 20 | 21 | 22 | 23 |
| 24 | 25 | 26 | 27 | 28 |   |   |

●:3  ◐:10  ○:18  ◑:26

### March

| S | M | T | W | T | F | S |
|---|---|---|---|---|---|---|
|   |   |   |   |   | 1 | 2 |
| 3 | 4 | 5 | 6 | 7 | 8 | 9 |
| 10 | 11 | 12 | 13 | 14 | 15 | 16 |
| 17 | 18 | 19 | 20 | 21 | 22 | 23 |
| 24 | 25 | 26 | 27 | 28 | 29 | 30 |
| 31 |   |   |   |   |   |   |

●:4  ◐:11  ○:20  ◑:27

### April

| S | M | T | W | T | F | S |
|---|---|---|---|---|---|---|
|   | 1 | 2 | 3 | 4 | 5 | 6 |
| 7 | 8 | 9 | 10 | 11 | 12 | 13 |
| 14 | 15 | 16 | 17 | 18 | 19 | 20 |
| 21 | 22 | 23 | 24 | 25 | 26 | 27 |
| 28 | 29 | 30 |   |   |   |   |

●:3  ◐:10  ○:18  ◑:25

### May

| S | M | T | W | T | F | S |
|---|---|---|---|---|---|---|
|   |   |   | 1 | 2 | 3 | 4 |
| 5 | 6 | 7 | 8 | 9 | 10 | 11 |
| 12 | 13 | 14 | 15 | 16 | 17 | 18 |
| 19 | 20 | 21 | 22 | 23 | 24 | 25 |
| 26 | 27 | 28 | 29 | 30 | 31 |   |

●:2  ◐:10  ○:18  ◑:25

### June

| S | M | T | W | T | F | S |
|---|---|---|---|---|---|---|
|   |   |   |   |   |   | 1 |
| 2 | 3 | 4 | 5 | 6 | 7 | 8 |
| 9 | 10 | 11 | 12 | 13 | 14 | 15 |
| 16 | 17 | 18 | 19 | 20 | 21 | 22 |
| 23 | 24 | 25 | 26 | 27 | 28 | 29 |
| 30 |   |   |   |   |   |   |

●:1  ◐:9  ○:16  ◑:23  ●:30

### July

| S | M | T | W | T | F | S |
|---|---|---|---|---|---|---|
|   | 1 | 2 | 3 | 4 | 5 | 6 |
| 7 | 8 | 9 | 10 | 11 | 12 | 13 |
| 14 | 15 | 16 | 17 | 18 | 19 | 20 |
| 21 | 22 | 23 | 24 | 25 | 26 | 27 |
| 28 | 29 | 30 | 31 |   |   |   |

◐:8  ○:16  ◑:22  ●:30

### August

| S | M | T | W | T | F | S |
|---|---|---|---|---|---|---|
|   |   |   |   | 1 | 2 | 3 |
| 4 | 5 | 6 | 7 | 8 | 9 | 10 |
| 11 | 12 | 13 | 14 | 15 | 16 | 17 |
| 18 | 19 | 20 | 21 | 22 | 23 | 24 |
| 25 | 26 | 27 | 28 | 29 | 30 | 31 |

◐:7  ○:14  ◑:20  ●:28

### September

| S | M | T | W | T | F | S |
|---|---|---|---|---|---|---|
| 1 | 2 | 3 | 4 | 5 | 6 | 7 |
| 8 | 9 | 10 | 11 | 12 | 13 | 14 |
| 15 | 16 | 17 | 18 | 19 | 20 | 21 |
| 22 | 23 | 24 | 25 | 26 | 27 | 28 |
| 29 | 30 |   |   |   |   |   |

◐:5  ○:12  ◑:19  ●:27

### October

| S | M | T | W | T | F | S |
|---|---|---|---|---|---|---|
|   |   | 1 | 2 | 3 | 4 | 5 |
| 6 | 7 | 8 | 9 | 10 | 11 | 12 |
| 13 | 14 | 15 | 16 | 17 | 18 | 19 |
| 20 | 21 | 22 | 23 | 24 | 25 | 26 |
| 27 | 28 | 29 | 30 | 31 |   |   |

◐:5  ○:11  ◑:19  ●:27

### November

| S | M | T | W | T | F | S |
|---|---|---|---|---|---|---|
|   |   |   |   |   | 1 | 2 |
| 3 | 4 | 5 | 6 | 7 | 8 | 9 |
| 10 | 11 | 12 | 13 | 14 | 15 | 16 |
| 17 | 18 | 19 | 20 | 21 | 22 | 23 |
| 24 | 25 | 26 | 27 | 28 | 29 | 30 |

◐:3  ○:10  ◑:17  ●:25

### December

| S | M | T | W | T | F | S |
|---|---|---|---|---|---|---|
| 1 | 2 | 3 | 4 | 5 | 6 | 7 |
| 8 | 9 | 10 | 11 | 12 | 13 | 14 |
| 15 | 16 | 17 | 18 | 19 | 20 | 21 |
| 22 | 23 | 24 | 25 | 26 | 27 | 28 |
| 29 | 30 | 31 |   |   |   |   |

◐:3  ○:9  ◑:17  ●:25

# PEOPLE IN HIGH OFFICE

**Franklin D. Roosevelt**
President - Democratic Party
March 4, 1933 - April 12, 1945

Born January 30, 1882, and commonly known by his initials FDR, Roosevelt served as the 32$^{nd}$ President of the United States until his death on April 12, 1945.

### 73$^{rd}$ & 74$^{th}$ United States Congress

| | |
|---|---|
| Vice President | John Nance Garner |
| Chief Justice | Charles Evans Hughes |
| Speaker of the House | Henry Thomas Rainey |
| Senate Majority Leader | Joseph Taylor Robinson |

*U.S. Flag - 48 stars (1912-1959)*

United Kingdom

Monarch
**King George V**

May 6, 1910
- January 20, 1936

Prime Minister
**Ramsey MacDonald**
National Government
June 5, 1929
- June 7, 1935

Prime Minister
**Stanley Baldwin**
Conservative Party
June 7, 1935
- May 28, 1937

Australia

Canada

Ireland

Prime Minister
**Joseph Lyons**
United Australia Party
January 6, 1932
- April 7, 1939

Prime Minister
**Richard Bedford Bennett**
Conservative Party
August 7, 1930
- October 23, 1935

President Executive Council
**Éamon de Valera**
Fianna Fáil
March 9, 1932
- December 29, 1937

Argentina

President
Agustín Pedro Justo (1932-1938)

Brazil

President
Getúlio Vargas (1930-1945)

China

Premier
Wang Jingwei (1932-1935)
Chiang Kai-shek (1935-1938)

Cuba

President
Carlos Mendieta (1934-1935)
José Agripino Barnet (1935-1936)

Egypt

Prime Minister
Muhammad Tawfiq Nasim Pasha (1934-1936)

France

President
Albert Lebrun (1932-1940)

Germany

Führer
Adolf Hitler (1934-1945)

India

Viceroy and Governor-General of India
Freeman Freeman-Thomas (1931-1936)

Italy

Prime Minister
Benito Mussolini (1922-1943)

Japan

Prime Minister
Keisuke Okada (1934-1936)

Mexico

President
Lázaro Cárdenas (1934-1940)

New Zealand

Prime Minister
George Forbes (1930-1935)
Michael Joseph Savage (1935-1940)

Russia

Communist Party Leader
Joseph Stalin (1922-1952)

South Africa

Prime Minister
James Barry Munnik Hertzog (1924-1939)

Spain

Prime Minister
Alejandro Lerroux (1934-1935)
Joaquín Chapaprieta (1935)
Manuel Portela Valladares (1935-1936)

Turkey

Prime Minister
İsmet İnönü (1925-1937)

# AMERICAN NEWS & EVENTS

## JAN

| | |
|---|---|
| 1 | The Orange Bowl, Sun Bowl, and Sugar Bowl college football games are all played for the first time. They are won by Bucknell (Orange Bowl), El Paso (Sun Bowl), and Tulane (Sugar Bowl). |
| 3 | The trial of Richard Hauptmann, accused of the kidnapping and murder of the 20-month-old son of aviator Charles Lindbergh and his wife Anne Morrow Lindbergh, begins in Flemington, New Jersey. *Follow up: Dubbed the "Trial of the Century," Hauptmann was found guilty of first-degree murder and sentenced to death on February 13, 1935. Despite his conviction he continued to profess his innocence but all appeals failed. He was executed in the electric chair at New Jersey State Prison on April 3, 1936.* |
| 4 | Dry Tortugas National Park, preserving Fort Jefferson and the several Dry Tortugas islands (the westernmost and most isolated of the Florida Keys), is established. *Fun facts: Fort Jefferson, a former military coastal fortress, is the largest brick masonry structure in the United States. It covers 16 acres and is made with over 16 million bricks.* |
| 4 | Bob Hope makes his first appearance on network radio as part of the cast of "The Intimate Revue." |

January 12: Amelia Earhart becomes the first person to fly solo from Hawaii to the U.S. mainland. The 2,408-mile flight from Honolulu to Oakland, California, took her 18 hours and 17 minutes. *Photo: Amelia Earhart, greeted by a crowd of some 5,000 people, is showered with flowers after landing at Oakland Airport.*

| | |
|---|---|
| 16 | The FBI kills Fred Barker and his mother Kate "Ma" Barker, members of the Barker-Karpis Gang, after a four-hour shootout near Lake Weir in Florida. |

| | |
|---|---|
| 19 | Coopers Inc. sells the world's first men's briefs, dubbed the "jockey," at Marshall Field's department store in Chicago, Illinois. *Fun fact: Over 30,000 pairs were sold within three months of their introduction.* |
| 24 | Canned beer goes on sale to the public for the first time in Richmond, Virginia. Made by the Gottfried Krueger Brewing Company, in partnership with the American Can Company, the 2,000 cans of Krueger's Cream Ale and Krueger's Finest Beer are well received by drinkers, driving Krueger to give the green light to further production. |

January 28: Pennsylvania Railroad 4800, the first GG1-class electric locomotive, inaugurates electric passenger service between Washington, D.C. and Philadelphia by pulling a charter train for railroad and government officials; on the return trip 4800 sets a speed record of 102 mph outside of Landover, Maryland. Regular passenger service on the line begins on February 10, 1935. *Photo: Pennsylvania Railroad 4800, nicknamed "Old Rivets," circa 1935.*

| | |
|---|---|
| 1 | The March of Time newsreel series, sponsored by Time Inc., is launched and debuts in over 500 in movie theaters. |
| 9 | The U.S. Figure Skating championships are held New Haven, Connecticut; Robin Lee wins the men's competition, and Maribel Vinson the ladies. |
| 12 | The USS Macon, the U.S. Navy's last great airship, is damaged in a storm and crashes into Pacific Ocean off Monterey Bay. Fortunately, due to the warm conditions and the introduction of life jackets and inflatable rafts, only two of the 83 men aboard the craft are killed. |
| 13 | The first surgical operation for relief of angina pectoris is carried out by Claude Beck in Cleveland, Ohio. |
| 22 | To prevent President Roosevelt and his family from having their sleep disturbed, Eugene L. Vidal, director of air commerce, issues an order making it illegal for aircraft to fly over the White House. |

| | |
|---|---|
| 22 | The comedy drama film "The Little Colonel," starring Shirley Temple, Lionel Barrymore and Bill Robinson, premieres. It features the first interracial dance pairing in Hollywood history. *NB: The staircase tap dance between Robinson and Temple was so controversial it was cut out in the Southern United States.* |
| 23 | The highly acclaimed Mickey Mouse cartoon "The Band Concert" is released by United Artists. *NB: "The Band Concert" was the first in the Mickey Mouse series of shorts to be produced in color.* |

February 27: The 7th Academy Awards ceremony, honoring the best films for 1934, is held at the Biltmore Hotel in Los Angeles, California. Hosted by Irvin S. Cobb, the winners include Frank Capra's romantic comedy "It Happened One Night," Clark Gable, and Claudette Colbert. *Fun fact: "It Happened One Night" became the first of three movies to date to sweep the top five awards: Best Picture, Best Director, Best Actor, Best Actress, and Best Screenplay. The other two are "One Flew Over the Cuckoo's Nest" (1976), and "The Silence of the Lambs" (1992). Photos: Best Actor Clark Gable / Best Actress Claudette Colbert (receiving her Oscar from presenter and Special Award winner Shirley Temple).*

| | |
|---|---|
| 28 | Nylon is synthesized for the first time by Gérard Berchet (working under the direction of Dr. Wallace H. Carothers) at DuPont's research facility in Wilmington, Delaware. |

**MAR**

| | |
|---|---|
| 2 | Porky Pig makes his debut in the Merrie Melodies short "I Haven't Got a Hat." |
| 6 | Czechoslovakian born Frank Bartell sets a new human-powered land speed record of 80.584 mph along a blocked-off boulevard on the outskirts of Los Angeles. |
| 19 | After rumors that a black Puerto Rican teenager has been brutally beaten by staff at a five and dime store in Harlem, New York City, the "first modern race riot" breaks out; 3 people are killed, hundreds injured, and an estimated $2 million in damage is caused to local property. |

| | |
|---|---|
| 1 | The North American NA-16, the first trainer aircraft built by North American Aviation and a prototype of the North American T-6 Texan, is flown for the first time by test pilot Eddie Allen at Dandalk, Maryland. |
| 6 | Harlem Globetrotter Harold "Bunny" Levitt makes a world record 499 consecutive basketball free throws at a YMCA carnival in Chicago. The 5ft 4in Levitt then proceeds to sink 371 more in a row before stopping. *Fun facts: Levitt's consecutive free throw record stood until 1975 when Ted St. Martin increased it to 1238. St. Martin, who never made the NBA or even played college ball, further increased the record to 5221 in 1996.* |

April 14: Dust Bowl: The great Black Sunday dust storm (made famous by Woody Guthrie in his "dust bowl ballads") sweeps the Oklahoma and Texas panhandles. *NB: The Black Sunday storm was one of the worst in American history and caused immense economic and agricultural damage. During the "Dust Bowl" era, from 1934 through 1938, there were 263 such dust storms recorded in Texas and Oklahoma alone. Photo: The Black Sunday storm hits Ulyssess, Kansas.*

| | |
|---|---|
| 15 | The Roerich Pact is signed in Washington, D.C. legally recognizing the preservation of cultural artefacts as more important than the destruction of their material for military use. |
| 16 | The radio comedy program "Fibber McGee and Molly," starring husband-and-wife team Jim Jordan and Marian Driscoll Jordan, debuts on NBC Blue. The show runs until October 2, 1959 (1611 episodes). |
| 19 | The classic horror film "Bride of Frankenstein," starring Boris Karloff, Colin Clive, and Elsa Lancaster is released. *NB: In 1998, "Bride of Frankenstein" was selected for preservation in the National Film Registry by the Library of Congress as being "culturally, historically, or aesthetically significant."* |

| | |
|---|---|
| 6 | President Roosevelt issues Executive Order 7034 establishing the Works Progress Administration (WPA). *NB: The WPA employed millions of jobseekers (mostly men who were not formally educated) to carry out public works projects, including the construction of public buildings and roads.* |
| 14 | The Griffith Observatory in Los Angeles is opened to the public. *NB: In its first five days of operation the observatory logs more than 13,000 visitors.* |
| 19 | The National Football League adopts a plan for a college player draft to begin in 1936. Proposed by Bert Bell, the co-owner of the Philadelphia Eagles and future NFL commissioner, the plan calls for teams to select players in inverse order of their finish the previous season. |
| 24 | The first night game in Major League Baseball history is played at Crosley Field in Cincinnati; the Reds defeat the Phillies 2-1. |

May 25: Jesse Owens sets five world records, and equals another, in the space of 45 minutes at the Big Ten Track and Field Championships in Ann Arbor, Michigan. The 21-year-old Ohio State sophomore ties the world record in the 100-yard dash (9.4 seconds) and then sets new world records in the long jump (26 feet 8¼ inches), the 220-yard dash (20.3 seconds), and the 220 low hurdles (22.6 seconds). World records times are also set for the 200-meter dash (during the 220-yard dash) and 200-meter low hurdles (during the 220-yard low hurdles). *Photo: Jesse Owens breaking the world long jump record at the Big Ten Championships.*

| | |
|---|---|
| 25 | Babe Ruth hits three home runs at Forbes Field in Pittsburgh, Pennsylvania, to bring his career tally to 714, a Major League record which stands until 1974. |
| 27 | Schechter Poultry Corp. v. United States: The Supreme Court declares that President Roosevelt's National Industrial Recovery Act, a major component of the New Deal, is unconstitutional. |

# MAY

| | |
|---|---|
| 31 | Nebraska's Deadliest Flood: Torrential rain in eastern Colorado and southwestern Nebraska causes the usually peaceful Republican River to flood. By the time the waters subside two days later as many as 135 people have been killed and the flooding has resulted in many millions of dollars' worth of damage; a total of 341 miles of highway and 307 bridges are destroyed. |
| 31 | The 20th Century-Fox Film Corporation is founded following a merger between 20th Century Pictures, Inc. and the Fox Film Corporation. |

# JUN

| | |
|---|---|
| 2 | Forty-year-old future Baseball Hall of Fame slugger Babe Ruth announces his retirement. |
| 10 | William G. Wilson (known as Bill W.) and Dr. Robert Smith (known as Dr. Bob) found Alcoholics Anonymous in Akron, Ohio (date of Smith's last drink). |
| 12 | Senator Huey Long of Louisiana, in an attempt to require Senate confirmation of the National Recovery Administration's senior employees, filibusters the New Deal legislation with a 15½ hour-long speech. |
| 12 | Conrad Bahr and George Pfefferle file a U.S. patent for an adjustable ratcheting torque wrench; the patent is granted on March 16, 1937. |

June 13: James J. Braddock upsets defending champion Max Baer, in a 15 round unanimous points decision, to win the NYSAC, NBA, and The Ring world heavyweight titles at Madison Square Garden Bowl in Queens, New York. *Photo: 10-to-1 underdog Jimmy Braddock (left) and Max Baer square off for photographers before the fight.*

## JUN

| | |
|---|---|
| 25 | Future world heavyweight boxing champion Joe Louis wins his 20th straight fight with a 6th round knockout of Primo Carnera, the former champion, at Yankee Stadium in New York City. |
| 26 | The National Youth Administration (NYA), focusing on providing work and education for Americans between the ages of 16 and 25, is established. |
| 27 | Irish wrestler Danno O'Mahoney beats Jim Londos at Boston's Fenway Park to win the New York State Athletic Commission World Heavyweight Championship. |
| 28 | The government reveals a plan to construct a massive underground vault at Fort Knox, Kentucky, to house the nation's gold reserves. |

## JUL

| | |
|---|---|
| 2 | Great Britain's amateur boxing team defeats the United States 8-3 in the first International Golden Gloves tournament. Held at Yankee Stadium in New York City, the bouts draw a crowd of 48,000, a record for an amateur card in the U.S. |
| 5 | The National Labor Relations Act is signed into law by President Roosevelt, guaranteeing the right of private sector employees to organize into trade unions, engage in collective bargaining, and take collective action such as strikes. |
| 5 | For the first time in Major League Baseball history brothers on opposing teams hit home runs; Tony Cuccinello (Brooklyn Dodgers) and Al Cuccinello (New York Giants) - the Dodgers beat the Giants 14-4. |
| 16 | The world's first parking meter, known as Park-O-Meter No.1, is installed on the southeast corner of First Street and Robinson Avenue in Oklahoma City, Oklahoma. |
| 17 | Variety magazine prints its famous, much-replicated, "Sticks Nix Hick Pix" headline. The accompanying article, based on an interview with theatre operator Joe Kinsky, claims that "Farmers are not interested in farming pictures." |
| 26 | Anti-Nazi demonstrators board the German luxury liner SS Bremen docked in New York Harbor, tear the Nazi swastika flag from its foremast, and then throw it into the Hudson River. |
| 27 | The Federal Writers' Project is created to provide jobs for out-of-work writers and to develop a history and overview of the United States. *NB: The project was dissolved in 1943.* |

## AUG

| | |
|---|---|
| 2 | The USS Philadelphia, a gunboat of the Continental Navy sunk on October 11, 1776, at the battle the Battle of Valcour Island during the American Revolutionary War, is raised to the surface of Lake Champlain and salvaged. *NB: Philadelphia and her associated artifacts are now part of the permanent collection of the National Museum of American History in Washington, D.C.* |
| 3 | 25,000 New Yorkers march down Harlem's Lenox Avenue to protest Fascist Italy's plans to invade Abyssinia (Ethiopia). |
| 5 | The Leo Burnett Advertising Agency is founded in Chicago, Illinois. *NB: The company today has 85 offices worldwide and over 9,000 employees.* |

16

August 13: The first Transcontinental Roller Derby, the brainchild of sports promoter Leo Seltzer, opens at the Coliseum in Chicago. Watched by more than 20,000 people, the 25 teams have to skate 3,000 miles around the track, a distance equal to that between San Diego and New York City. *Follow up: The roller derby was won by teammates Clarice Martin and Bernie McKay over a month later, on Sunday, September 22, in a time of 493 hours and 12 minutes. Photo: The inaugural Transcontinental Roller Derby at the Chicago Coliseum.*

| | |
|---|---|
| 14 | President Roosevelt signs the Social Security Act into law to provide insurance and welfare programs for elderly, unemployed and disadvantaged Americans. |
| 15 | Humorist Will Rogers and aviator Wiley Post (the first pilot to fly solo around the world) are killed when Post's aircraft crashes on take-off near Point Barrow, Alaska. |
| 29 | The musical comedy film "Top Hat," the most successful picture of Fred Astaire and Ginger Rogers' partnership, premieres in New York City. *NB: In 1990, "Top Hat" was selected for preservation in the National Film Registry by the Library of Congress as being "culturally, historically, or aesthetically significant."* |
| 31 | As part of American non-interventionism in the face of growing tensions in Europe, Congress passes the first Neutrality Act prohibiting the export of "arms, ammunition, and implements of war" from the U.S. to foreign nations at war. |

| | |
|---|---|
| 2 | Labor Day Hurricane: The strongest hurricane ever to strike the United States makes landfall in the Upper Florida Keys killing 423. It is a Category 5 storm with winds reaching 185 mph. *NB: The storm remained the strongest Atlantic hurricane at landfall, in terms of 1-minute sustained winds, until it was tied by Hurricane Dorian in 2019.* |

September 3: British racing driver Sir Malcolm Campbell becomes the first person to break the 300 mph barrier (establishing a new absolute land speed record of 301.337 mph) driving his Rolls Royce-powered car Blue Bird on the Bonneville Salt Flats in Utah. *Photo: Fifty-year-old Malcolm Campbell setting the land speed record at Bonneville in his 2,300 hp Campbell-Railton Blue Bird.*

| | |
|---|---|
| 3 | Andrew Varipapa breaks the world bowling record for ten games by scoring 2,652 points at the Lawler Brothers Academy in Brooklyn; his scores are 222, 267, 279, 255, 258, 279, 279, 299, 278, 236. |
| 8 | Physician Carl Weiss fatally wounds Louisiana Senator Huey Long with a single shot from a handgun at the Louisiana Capitol Building in Baton Rouge. Long's bodyguards respond by shooting Weiss and killing him instantly (an autopsy found that Weiss had been shot more than 60 times). Senator Long died at 4:10 a.m. on September 10, 31 hours after being shot. |
| 8 | Film director and musical choreographer Busby Berkeley is involved in three-car accident on Roosevelt Highway near Santa Monica. The accident kills two people and injures five, and leads to Berkeley being charged with second-degree murder. *Follow up: Two subsequent trials end with hung juries; he is acquitted in a third.* |
| 13 | Howard Hughes, flying the Hughes H-1 Racer, sets an airspeed record of 352.39 mph at Martin Field near Santa Ana, California. |
| 13 | A rockslide near the Niagara Falls Whirlpool Rapids Bridge destroys more than 200 feet of track and rail bed, forcing the Great Gorge Route, operated by the International Railway Company, to close for business. |
| 23 | The first victim of the Cleveland Torso Murderer, Edward Anthony Andrassy, is discovered. *NB: The murder began a 3-year series of killings and beheadings around the Kingsbury Run district of Cleveland, Ohio. The perpetrator was never apprehended.* |
| 24 | Mississippi's first rodeo, sponsored by rancher Samuel Hickman and drug store owner George Baylis, is held at the Columbia High School baseball field. *NB: The outdoor rodeo was recognized as the nation's first to be held at night under electric lights.* |

# SEP

| | |
|---|---|
| 30 | The Secretary of the Interior Harold L. Ickes formally dedicates the Boulder Dam during a ceremony attended by President Roosevelt. *Fun fact: During construction the dam was referred to as the Hoover Dam, after President Herbert Hoover, but was named the Boulder Dam by the Roosevelt administration. In 1947, the name Hoover Dam was restored by Congress.* |
| 30 | George Gershwin's opera "Porgy and Bess" premieres at the Colonial Theatre in Boston; 10 days later it opens on Broadway at the Alvin Theatre. |

# OCT

| | |
|---|---|
| 3 | The Hayden Planetarium, designed by architects Trowbridge & Livingston, opens in New York City. *Fun fact: In its first year the Hayden Planetarium drew over half a million visitors, as well as to more than 130,000 schoolchildren who were admitted free of charge.* |
| 7 | The Detroit Tigers defeat the Chicago Cubs, 4 games to 2, to win their first World Series Title. |
| 15 | The NHL's St. Louis Eagles, formerly the Ottawa Senators, folds after only one year. |

October 18: A 6.2 magnitude earthquake strikes Helena, the capital of Montana, with a maximum Mercalli intensity of VIII (Severe), causing widespread damage and two deaths. A high intensity aftershock claims an additional two lives on October 31. *Photo: A colorized view of the earthquake-damaged Nabisco factory in Helena, November 10, 1935.*

| | |
|---|---|
| 23 | Mobsters Dutch Schultz, Abe Landau, Otto Berman and Bernard "Lulu" Rosencrantz, are fatally shot by two Murder, Inc. hitmen, Charles "The Bug" Workman and Emanuel "Mendy" Weiss, at the Palace Chop House restaurant in Newark, New Jersey. |

| | |
|---|---|
| 5 | The Parker Brothers begin marketing Monopoly, their recently-acquired real estate game. |
| 8 | United Mine Workers leader, John L. Lewis, together with other labor union leaders, announce the creation of the Committee for Industrial Organization, a new group within the American Federation of Labor (AFL) charged with promoting the cause of industrial unionism in North America. |
| 8 | The historical drama film "Mutiny on the Bounty," directed by Frank Lloyd and starring Charles Laughton and Clark Gable, premieres in New York City. *NB: The movie received eight nominations at the 8th Academy Awards, winning one, Outstanding Production (Best Picture).* |

November 11: Explorer II, a manned high-altitude balloon, makes a record-breaking ascent to 72,395 ft over South Dakota. It's crew, Army Air Corps Captains Albert W. Stevens and Orvil A. Anderson, are sealed inside a spherical cabin and watched by a crowd of some 20,000 people. *NB: The success of the mission was much celebrated in the press and the aeronauts became national heroes. Both men were presented with the National Geographic Society's Hubbard Medal, the Army Air Corps Mackay Trophy, for the most meritorious flight of the year, and the Distinguished Flying Cross. Photos: Ballooning pioneers Orvil Anderson (left) and Albert Stevens / The Explorer II balloon shortly before its record-setting ascent.*

| | |
|---|---|
| 15 | A 700-strong mob lynches two African-American youths, 15-year-old Ernest Collins and 16-year-old Benny Mitchell, in Colorado County, Texas, after they allegedly admit to attacking and drowning 19-year-old Geraldine Kollmann. The next day, the county attorney publicly says that the lynchings are "an expression of the will of the people," and a local judge calls the lynchings "justice." No one is ever held accountable for their deaths. |

| 15 | The Historical Records Survey, part of the Works Progress Administration, is formed to survey and index historically significant records in state, county and local archives. |
| 15 | The MGM comedy film "A Night at the Opera," directed by Sam Wood and starring the Marx Brothers, is released. *NB: In 1993, "A Night at the Opera" was selected for preservation in the National Film Registry by the Library of Congress as being "culturally, historically, or aesthetically significant."* |

November 22: The fixed-winged seaplane China Clipper, crewed by pilot Edwin C. Musick and navigator Fred Noonan, takes off from Alameda, California, to deliver the first airmail cargo across the Pacific Ocean; the aircraft reaches its destination of Manila on November 29, and delivers over 110,000 pieces of mail. *Photo: Pan American Airways "China Clipper" over San Francisco at the beginning its 8,000-mile journey to deliver mail across the Pacific Ocean.*

# DEC

| 5 | Educator and government consultant Mary McLeod Bethune founds the National Council of Negro Women, a non-profit organisation aiming to advance the opportunities of African-American women and their families. |
| 9 | Investigative reporter Walter Liggett, midway through a crusade against the Farmer-Labor party for its perceived links with organized crime, is killed in a drive-by shooting outside his home in Minneapolis, Minnesota. *Follow up: Despite mobster Isadore Blumenfeld, commonly known as Kid Cann, being picked out as the shooter by Liggett's wife and several neighbors, he is acquitted.* |

December 9: The first Downtown Athletic Club Trophy, to recognize "the most valuable college football player east of the Mississippi," is awarded to University of Chicago halfback Jay Berwanger. *NB: After the death in October 1936 of the Downtown Athletic Club's athletic director John Heisman, the award was renamed the Heisman Trophy and broadened to include players west of the Mississippi. Photo: The winner of the first Heisman Trophy, Jay Berwanger, pictured with the bronze statue.*

| | |
|---|---|
| 17 | The Douglas Sleeper Transport, a prototype of the Douglas DC-3 airliner, makes its first flight at Santa Monica, California, with chief test pilot Carl Cover at the controls. |
| 26 | Shenandoah National Park, encompassing part of the Blue Ridge Mountains, is established in Virginia. |

# Worldwide News & Events

1. January 7: The Franco-Italian Agreement, designed to contain Hitler's ambitions in Europe, is signed in Rome by Italian premier Benito Mussolini and French Foreign Minister Pierre Laval.

2. January 13: A plebiscite in the Territory of the Saar Basin, governed by the United Kingdom and France since 1920 under a League of Nations mandate, shows that 90.3% of those voting wish to join Germany. *NB: The Territory of the Saar Basin was re-integrated into Germany on March 1, 1935.*

3. February 8: In the Turkish general election women are able to vote for the first time.

4. February 11: The temperature in Ifrane, Morocco, drops to -11.0°F (African record).

5. February 20: Danish-Norwegian explorer Caroline Mikkelsen lands on the Tryne Islands, becoming the first woman to set foot on Antarctica. *NB: Norwegian Ingrid Christensen landed at Scullin Monolith on January 30, 1937, and was the first woman to set foot on the Antarctic mainland.*

6. February 21: Rolls-Royce's PV-12 (Merlin) aircraft engine is flown for the first time in a Hawker Hart biplane at Hucknall Aerodrome near Nottingham, England. *Fun facts: By the time production of the engine ceased in 1950, 149,659 had been built.*

7. February 26: In Northamptonshire, England, Robert Watson-Watt and Arnold Wilkins demonstrate radar for the first time by bouncing radio signals off a Handley Page Heyford bomber and detecting them using two receiving antennae. *Follow up: Further development by Watson-Watt led to the British government commissioning an array of fixed radar towers, known as Chain Home, across the east and south coasts of England. NB: It was radar, more than anything else, that provided the vital advance information that saved the Royal Air Force (RAF) from defeat during the Battle of Britain in 1940. Photo: The Chain Home radar installation at Poling, Sussex, circa 1945.*

8. February 26: Nazi leader Adolf Hitler signs a secret decree authorizing the founding of the German air force, the Reich Luftwaffe, in violation of the 1919 Treaty of Versailles. Hermann Goering is appointed as its commander in chief.

| 9. | February 28: The Ladby Ship, the only Viking ship burial to be discovered in Denmark, is found near Kerteminde. It is believed to date back over 1,000 years. |
| 10. | March 1: Nikolaos Plastiras leads a Venizelist revolt in a coup against the People's Party government in Greece. The attempt is suppressed by March 11, and its leaders condemned to death for treason. |
| 11. | March 1: Following the February 8 general election in Turkey, the Republican People's Party leader İsmet İnönü is returned as the country's Prime Minister. |
| 12. | March 2: King Prajadhipok (Rama VII) of Siam abdicates his throne; he is succeeded by his 9-year-old-nephew Ananda Mahidol (Rama VIII). |
| 13. | March 8: Japan's most famous dog, Hachikō, dies on a street in Shibuya almost ten years after the death of his beloved owner. |
| 14. | March 12: A 30 mph speed limit is introduced for cars and motorcycles in built up areas across Britain. |
| 15. | March 16: Adolf Hitler announces German re-armament, and the reintroduction of conscription, in violation of the 1919 Treaty of Versailles. |
| 16. | March 16: Voluntary driving tests are introduced across the United Kingdom. |
| 17. | March 21: As requested by Reza Shah Pahlavi, the international community formally adopts the name "Iran" in place of the country's former name "Persia." |
| 18. | March 28: The influential Nazi propaganda film "Triumph of the Will," commissioned by Adolf Hitler and directed by Leni Riefenstahl, is released. It chronicles the 1934 Nazi Party Congress in Nuremberg which was attended by more than 700,000 Nazi supporters. |
| 19. | April 27: The Brussels International Exposition is held on the Heysel Plateau in Brussels, Belgium. It is the tenth world's fair hosted by Belgium, and it attracts some twenty million visitors before closing on November 6, 1935. |
| 20. | April 29: The first edition of the Vuelta a España begins in Madrid, Spain. The 14 stage, 2,119-mile bicycle race is won by Belgium's Gustaaf Deloor on May 15. *NB: The Vuelta a España has become one of the three bicycle race Grand Tours, alongside the Tour de France and the Giro d'Italia.* |

21. May 6: Large-scale events take place throughout the United Kingdom to celebrate King George V's Silver Jubilee. The celebrations include a carriage procession through London to St Paul's Cathedral for a national service of thanksgiving, before a return to Buckingham Palace where the King and Queen are joined by other members of the Royal Family on the balcony. *Photo: The Royal procession returning to Buckingham Palace from the thanksgiving service at St Paul's Cathedral.*

| 22. | May 13: British officer, diplomat, archaeologist and writer, Colonel T. E. Lawrence, better known as Lawrence of Arabia, is fatally injured in a motorcycle accident close to his cottage near Wareham in Dorset, England. He dies six days later. |
| 23. | May 15: The Moscow Metro, consisting of a single 6.8-mile line serving 13 stations, is opened to the public. *Fun fact: Today the Moscow Metro has over 200 stations and 235 miles of track.* |
| 24. | May 19: Cardinal John Fisher and statesman Sir Thomas More, both executed by British monarch King Henry VIII 400 years earlier in 1535, are canonized as saints by Pope Pius XI. |
| 25. | May 22: The British government announce that the RAF is to triple in size over the next two years to give it 1,500 aircraft by 1937 (the same number that Germany says it intends to have). |

26. May 29: The French transatlantic ocean liner SS Normandie sets out on her maiden voyage from Le Havre to New York. She arrives in New York in 4 days, 3 hours and 2 minutes, taking the westbound Blue Riband for the fastest transatlantic crossing; she also captures the eastbound Blue Riband on her return passage. *Fun facts: The SS Normandie was the largest and fastest passenger ship of her time, and remains the most powerful steam turbo-electric-propelled passenger ship ever built. Photo: The 79,280-ton SS Normandie, built in Saint-Nazaire, France, arriving in New York harbour, circa 1936.*

| 27. | May 31: A 7.7 magnitude earthquake hits Quetta in British India (now Pakistan) killing between 30,000 and 60,000 people. *NB: The Quetta earthquake was the most devastating to ever hit South Asia until the 2005 Kashmir earthquake which killed over 86,000 people.* |
| 28. | June 1: Compulsory driving tests are introduced in Britain for anyone who started driving on or after April 1, 1934. *Fun fact: The only person in the United Kingdom who is not required to have a licence in order to drive is the monarch.* |

| 29. | June 10: He-Umezu Agreement: A secret agreement between the Empire of Japan and the Republic of China is made, giving Japan virtual control over the Hebei Province (under the aegis of the East Hebei Autonomous Council). |
|---|---|
| 30. | June 12: The Chaco War between Paraguay and Bolivia, over the control of the northern part of the Gran Chaco region of South America (which was thought to be rich in oil), comes to an end. *NB: The war cost both nations dearly. Bolivia lost between 56,000 and 65,000 people, 2% of its population, and Paraguay lost about 36,000, 3% of its population.* |
| 31. | June 18: The Anglo-German Naval Agreement, decreeing that the size of the German navy in tonnage should be 35% that of the British navy, is signed in London by German diplomat Joachim von Ribbentrop and British Foreign Secretary Sir Samuel Hoare. *NB: Hitler denounces the agreement four years later on April 28, 1939.* |
| 32. | June 24: The "King of Tango," French-Argentine singer-songwriter Carlos Gardel, dies in a plane crash in Medellín, Colombia, aged 44. |

33. July 2: The Cunard White Star Line ocean liner RMS Mauretania (1906) departs Southampton for the last time to Metal Industries shipbreakers at Rosyth in Scotland. *NB: The demise of the beloved Mauretania was protested by many of her loyal passengers including President Franklin D. Roosevelt, who wrote a private letter against the scrapping. Fun facts: Mauretania was the world's largest ship until the launch of RMS Olympic in 1910. She notably captured the eastbound Blue Riband on her maiden return voyage in December 1907, then claimed the westbound Blue Riband during her 1909 season. She held both speed records for 20 years. Photo: Mauretania leaves Southampton for the last time to be broken up at Rosyth.*

| 34. | July 6: The Yangtze River floods the provinces of Hubei, Hunan, Jiangxi, Anhui, Jiangsu and Zhejiang in China; millions of people are displaced and 145,000 lose their lives. |
|---|---|
| 35. | July 6: The 14th Dalai Lama, Tenzin Gyatso, the foremost spiritual leader of the Gelug school of Tibetan Buddhism, is born in the Qinghai Province of China. |

36. July 12: After several months of rising tensions in Northern Ireland, rioting breaks out in Belfast following Orange Order parades; it is the worst violence seen in the city since Northern Ireland's foundation in 1922. *Follow up: The rioting continued until the end of August by which time eight Protestants and five Catholics had been killed, hundreds of people injured, and over 2,000 homes destroyed (almost all Catholic). Photo: Armed police on guard on the corner of York and Earl Street, Belfast, shortly after the riots.*

| | |
|---|---|
| 37. | July 13: In the United Kingdom, the official completion of London County Council's Becontree estate is celebrated with the ceremonial opening of Parsloes Park by MP Christopher Addison. Constructed between 1921 and 1935, it is the largest housing estate in the world and consists of some 25,736 council houses which are home to over 100,000 people. |
| 38. | July 20: A KLM Royal Dutch Airlines Douglas DC-2 aircraft, en route from Milan to Frankfurt, crashes into a Swiss mountain; all 13 people on board are killed. |
| 39. | July 22: "A Voz do Brasil" (The Voice of Brazil), the oldest radio program in Brazil and the longest-running in the Southern Hemisphere, hits the airwaves for the first time. |
| 40. | July 28: The 29th edition of the Tour de France, consisting of 21 stages over 2,696 miles, is won by Romain Maes of Belgium. *NB: This was the first Tour that had a stage finish and start in a city that was not in France (Geneva, Switzerland).* |
| 41. | July 30: Penguin Books is founded by Allen Lane and his brothers Richard and John, bringing high-quality paperback fiction and non-fiction to the mass market. |
| 42. | August 2: The U.K. Government of India Act 1935, making provision for the establishment of a "Federation of India" and the granting of a large measure of autonomy to the provinces of India, receives royal assent. |
| 43. | August 10 - September 1: The 3rd Venice International Film Festival takes place. The winners include Carmine Gallone's "Casta Diva" (Best Italian Film), Clarence Brown's "Anna Karenina" (Best Foreign Film), and Walt Disney's "The Band Concert" (Golden Medal). |
| 44. | August 13: A dam which forms part of the large hydroelectric reservoir of Molare, near Ovada, Italy, collapses following heavy rainfall; 110-115 people are killed. |

| 45. | August 16: Representatives of France, Britain and Italy meet in Paris in an attempt to negotiate a solution to the Abyssinia Crisis. The conference ends two days later with nothing resolved. |
|---|---|
| 46. | August 17. The Deaflympics, an international multi-sport event officially known as 4th International Games for the Deaf, is held at White City Stadium in London, England. Contested by 221 athletes from 12 nations, the event concludes a week later with Great Britain topping the medals table. |
| 47. | September: Rowntree's launches the "Chocolate Crisp" (later renamed Kit Kat) in London and throughout southern England. *Fun facts: Today, Kit Kats are made globally by Nestlé, with the exception of the U.S. where they are made by Hershey. Note: Hershey's and Nestlé's Kit Kats don't taste the same.* |
| 48. | September 11: The Irish-bred, English-trained Thoroughbred racehorse Bahram completes the English Triple Crown by finishing first in St. Leger at Doncaster; he had won both the 2,000 Guineas and Epsom Derby earlier in the year. |
| 49. | September 15: The Nuremberg Laws are enacted in Nazi Germany decreeing that those of Jewish blood should be ineligible for Reich citizenship, and forbidding marriages and intercourse between Germans and Jews. *NB: The laws were expanded on November 26, 1935, to include Romani and Black people but, out of foreign policy concerns, prosecutions did not commence until after the 1936 Summer Olympics in Berlin.* |
| 50. | September 16 - 21: The First International Congress for the Unity of Science is held at the Sorbonne in Paris. |
| 51. | September 19: Russian miner Aleksey Stakhanov (allegedly) sets a new record by mining 227 tonnes of coal in a single shift. *NB: His example was held up in Russian newspapers and posters as a model for others to follow to increase productivity. He even appeared on the cover of Time magazine in the United States.* |
| 52. | October 1: Thailand ceases to recognize polygamy in civil law. |
| 53. | October 3: Second Italo-Ethiopian War: Two hundred thousand soldiers of the Italian Army, commanded by Marshal Emilio De Bono, invade Abyssinia. |
| 54. | October 4: Luna Park, one of the most famous landmarks in Sydney, Australia, opens to the public. |
| 55. | October 7: In Geneva, Britain and twelve other nations bind themselves to the application of financial and economic sanctions against Italy over Abyssinia. |
| 56. | October 10: General Giorgios Kondylis, in favor of restoring the Greek monarchy, engineers a successful military coup d'etat in Greece. |
| 57. | October 14: William Lyon Mackenzie King is elected as the Prime Minister of Canada for the third time, five years after losing power in the previous federal election. |
| 58. | October 18 - 27: The Jérémie hurricane, also known as the Haiti hurricane, impacts Haiti, Jamaica, Cuba, Honduras and Nicaragua; over 2,000 people are killed. |
| 59. | October 20: Communist forces end their Long March, after retreating thousands of miles through western and central China, to convene at their new Communist base of operations at Yan'an in Shaanxi, China. *NB: The most famous of the marches was undertaken by the First Red Army under Mao Zedong. His leadership during the retreat brought him immense prestige and support, and marked the beginning of his ascent to primacy within the Chinese Communist Party.* |
| 60. | November 1: The Premier of the Republic of China, Wang Jingwei, is seriously wounded during an assassination attempt by notorious gangster Wang Yaqiao. |
| 61. | November 3: Korean athlete Sohn Kee-chung breaks the world marathon record with a time of 2h:26m:42s in Tokyo, Japan. *NB: The record remained unbroken until Sohn's own trainee, Suh Yun-Bok, won the 1947 Boston Marathon in a time of 2h:25m:39s.* |

62. November 3: Eleven years after Greece voted to become a republic, a monarchy referendum sees a 98% vote to restore the exiled King George II to the throne.

63. November 6: The RAF's prototype Hawker Hurricane fighter aircraft makes its maiden flight at Brooklands in Surrey, England.

64. November 14: British General election: Prime Minister Stanley Baldwin (Conservative Party) is returned to office at the head of the National Government with a large, albeit reduced, majority. *NB: Although Baldwin retired two years later, the 1935 House remained in power until 1945 due to WWII. Photo: Future Prime Minister Winston Churchill (with his wife Clementine) pictured in Waltham Abbey, part of his Epping constituency, on the campaign trail for the 1935 General Election.*

65. November 15: The Commonwealth of Philippines, an unincorporated territory of the United States, is inaugurated with Manuel L. Quezon as its President.

66. November 25: The International Institute for Social History (IISG) is founded in Amsterdam, Netherlands.

67. November 29: Austrian Physicist Erwin Schrödinger publishes his famous thought experiment "Schrödinger's cat," a paradox that illustrates the problem of the Copenhagen interpretation of quantum mechanics.

68. December 6: Michael Joseph Savage becomes the first Labour government Prime Minister of New Zealand.

69. December 8: In an attempt to end the Abyssinian Crisis, French Foreign Minister Pierre Laval and British Foreign Secretary Sir Samuel Hoare concoct the Hoare-Laval Pact, a suggested plan to partition Abyssinia, handing much of its territory to Italy. *Follow up: The proposal was met with outrage in Britain and France and never went into effect. Hoare and Laval both later resigned.*

70. December 10: James Chadwick is awarded the Nobel Prize in Physics for his discovery of the neutron in 1932. *Fun fact: In 2014, Chadwick's Nobel medal and diploma was sold by Sotheby's auction house in New York for $329,000.*

71. December 10: The Nobel Prize for Chemistry is awarded to the husband-and-wife team of Irène and Frédéric Joliot-Curie for their discovery of induced radioactivity.
72. December 10: A SABENA Savoia-Marchetti S.73 airliner crashes while on an international scheduled flight from Brussels to London. All eleven passengers and crew are killed.
73. December 12: The Lebensborn program, in support of Nazi eugenics, is founded by Heinrich Himmler in Germany.
74. December 15: In major upset, Dutch grand master Max Euwe becomes World Chess Champion after defeating Alexander Alekhine of Russia, 15½ - 14½, in the Netherlands.
75. December 27: In Germany, Regina Jonas becomes the first the first woman to be ordained as a rabbi.

# BIRTHS

## American Personalities

## BORN IN 1935

**Floyd Patterson**
*b. January 4, 1935*
*d. May 11, 2006*
Boxer who twice reigned as the world
heavyweight champion.

**Elvis Presley**
*b. January 8, 1935*
*d. August 16, 1977*
Singer and actor who is one of the best-
selling music artists of all time.

**A. J. Foyt**
*b. January 16, 1935*

Racing driver who was the first four-time
winner of the Indianapolis 500.

**Dorothy Provine**
*b. January 20, 1935*
*d. April 25, 2010*
Singer, dancer and actress.

**Don Maynard**
*b. January 25, 1935*
*d. January 10, 2022*
Football wide receiver inducted into the Pro
Football Hall of Fame in 1987.

**Gene Vincent**
*b. February 11, 1935*
*d. October 12, 1971*
Musician inducted into both the Rock & Roll
and Rockabilly Halls of Fame.

**Mickey Wright**
*b. February 14, 1935*
*d. February 17, 2020*
Golfer inducted into the World Golf Hall of
Fame in 1964.

**Sonny Bono**
*b. February 16, 1935*
*d. January 5, 1998*
Singer, songwriter, actor and politician.

**Sally Jessy Raphael**
*b. February 25, 1935*

Tabloid talk show host.

**Judd Hirsch**
*b. March 15, 1935*

Multi award winning actor.

**Herb Alpert**
*b. March 31, 1935*

Trumpeter and bandleader who has sold an estimated 72 million records worldwide.

**Bobby Vinton**
*b. April 16, 1935*

Singer-songwriter and occasional actor.

**Charles Grodin**
*b. April 21, 1935*
*d. May 18, 2021*
Actor, comedian, author and television talk show host.

**Doug McClure**
*b. May 11, 1935*
*d. February 5, 1995*
Actor best known for his role as Trampas in the television series The Virginian.

**David Hartman**
*b. May 19, 1935*

Journalist and actor best known as the first host of ABC's Good Morning America.

**Lee Meriwether**
*b. May 27, 1935*

Actress, former model, and winner of the 1955 Miss America pageant.

**Len Dawson**
*b. June 20, 1935*
*d. August 24, 2022*
Football quarterback inducted into the Pro Football Hall of Fame in 1987.

**Harrison Schmitt**
*b. July 3, 1935*

Geologist, astronaut, university professor, and former senator from New Mexico.

**Jack Kemp**
*b. July 13, 1935*
*d. May 2, 2009*
Republican Party politician and professional football player.

**Ken Kercheval**
*b. July 15, 1935*
*d. April 21, 2019*
Actor best known for his role as Cliff Barnes on the television series Dallas.

**Diahann Carroll**
*b. July 17, 1935*
*d. October 4, 2019*
Actress, singer, model and activist.

**Tenley Albright**
*b. July 18, 1935*

Olympic gold medal winning figure skater and surgeon.

**Geoffrey Lewis**
*b. July 31, 1935*
*d. April 7, 2015*
Actor who appeared in more than 200 films and television shows.

**Ron Paul**
*b. August 20, 1935*

Author, activist, physician and retired politician.

**Geraldine Ferraro**
*b. August 26, 1935*
*d. March 26, 2011*
Politician, diplomat and attorney.

**Frank Robinson**
*b. August 31, 1935*
*d. February 7, 2019*
Baseball outfielder and manager elected to the Baseball Hall of Fame in 1982.

**Jim Taylor**
*b. September 20, 1935*
*d. October 13, 2018*
Football fullback inducted into the Pro Football Hall of Fame in 1976.

**Jerry Lee Lewis**
*b. September 29, 1935*
*d. October 28, 2022*
Pianist, singer and songwriter.

**Johnny Mathis**

*b. September 30, 1935*

Singer who has sold over 360 million records worldwide.

**Charles Duke**

*b. October 3, 1935*

Astronaut, USAF officer and test pilot who was the 10th person to walk on the Moon.

**Bruno Sammartino**

*b. October 6, 1935*
*d. April 18, 2018*

Wrestler who reigned as the WWWF World Heavyweight Champion for 2,803 days.

**Bobby Morrow**

*b. October 15, 1935*
*d. May 30, 2020*

Sprinter who won three gold medals at the 1956 Olympics.

**Peter Boyle**

*b. October 18, 1935*
*d. December 12, 2006*
Actor.

**Charles Koch**

*b. November 1, 1935*

Billionaire businessman who is co-owner, chairman, and CEO of Koch Industries.

**Diane Ladd**
*b. November 29, 1935*

Actress who has appeared in over 200 films
and television shows.

**Woody Allen**
*b. November 30, 1935*

Filmmaker, actor and comedian.

**Lee Remick**
*b. December 14, 1935*
*d. July 2, 1991*
Actress and singer.

**Phil Donahue**
*b. December 21, 1935*

Media personality, writer, film producer and
creator / host of The Phil Donahue Show.

**Paul Hornung**
*b. December 23, 1935*
*d. November 13, 2020*
Football halfback and kicker inducted into
the Pro Football Hall of Fame in 1986.

**Sandy Koufax**
*b. December 30, 1935*

Baseball pitcher elected to the Baseball
Hall of Fame in 1972.

# Notable American Deaths

| | |
|---|---|
| Jan 15 | Marion Howard Brazier (b. September 6, 1850) - Journalist, editor, author and clubwoman. |
| Jan 16 | Kate "Ma" Barker (b. Arizona Donnie Clark; October 8, 1873) - The mother of four criminal sons who was killed after a lengthy gunfight with the FBI in Ocklawaha, Florida. |
| Jan 16 | Frederick George Barker (b. December 12, 1901) - Criminal who, along with Alvin Karpis, co-founded the Barker-Karpis gang which committed numerous robberies, murders and kidnappings during the 1930s. |
| Jan 19 | Lloyd Vernon Hamilton (b. August 19, 1891) - Film comedian, best remembered for his work during the silent era, who was honored with a star on the Hollywood Walk of Fame in 1960. |
| Feb 5 | Jackson Whipps Showalter (b. February 5, 1859) - Five-time American chess champion. |
| Feb 9 | Thomas Clay McDowell (b. March 9, 1866) - Thoroughbred racehorse owner / breeder and trainer, best known for his colt Alan-a-Dale (winner of the 1902 Kentucky Derby). |
| Mar 2 | Samuel Sachs (b. July 28, 1851) - Investment banker who co-founded Goldman Sachs with father-in-law Marcus Goldman. |
| Mar 6 | Oliver Wendell Holmes Jr. (b. March 8, 1841) - Jurist who served as an associate justice of the Supreme Court (1902-1932). |
| Mar 12 | Mihajlo Idvorski Pupin (b. October 4, 1858) - Serbian-American physicist, physical chemist and philanthropist. |
| Mar 23 | Florence E. Moore (b. November 13, 1886) - Vaudeville, Broadway and silent film actress. |
| Apr 2 | Benjamin "Bennie" Moten (b. November 13, 1893) - Jazz pianist and band leader of the Kansas City Orchestra. |
| Apr 6 | Edwin Arlington Robinson (b. December 22, 1869) - Poet and playwright who won the Pulitzer Prize for Poetry on three occasions, and was nominated for the Nobel Prize in Literature four times. |
| Apr 8 | Adolph Simon Ochs (b. March 12, 1858) - Newspaper publisher and former owner of The New York Times. |
| Apr 11 | Anna Katharine Green (b. November 11, 1846) - Poet and novelist who was one of the first writers of detective fiction in America. |
| Apr 18 | Arthur Grosvenor Daniells (b. September 28, 1858) - Seventh-day Adventist minister and administrator, and longest serving president of the General Conference (1901-1922). |
| Apr 29 | Leroy Carr (b. March 27, 1904) - Blues singer, songwriter and pianist who was inducted into the Blues Hall of Fame in 1982. |
| May 3 | Jessie Willcox Smith (b. September 6, 1863) - Artist best remembered for her illustrations, often featuring children, for numerous popular magazines, advertising campaigns, and children's books. |
| May 6 | Bronson Murray Cutting (b. June 23, 1888) - Republican Senator from New Mexico (1927-1935) who helped establish freedom of the press. |
| May 11 | Edward Herbert Thompson (b. September 28, 1857) - Archaeologist who revealed much about the Mayan civilization from his exploration of the city and religious shrine of Chichen Itza in Yucatán, Mexico. |

May 21: Laura Jane Addams (b. September 6, 1860) - Activist, reformer, social worker, sociologist, public administrator, philosopher, author and Nobel Peace Prize recipient (1931) who and was an important leader in the history of social work and women's suffrage in the United States.

In 1889, Addams notably co-founded Chicago's Hull House, one of America's most famous settlement houses, providing extensive social services to poor, largely immigrant families. *Photo: Jane Addams, circa 1870s.*

| | |
|---|---|
| Jun 19 | Charles Henry Niehaus (b. January 24, 1855) - Sculptor whose monuments can be found in many American cities. |
| Jul 2 | Henry M. O'Day (b. July 8, 1859) - Major League Baseball pitcher, manager, umpire and scout, nicknamed "The Reverend," who was inducted into the Baseball Hall of Fame in 2013. |
| Jul 7 | George Keller (b. December 15, 1842) - Architect and engineer. Keller's most famous projects are the Soldiers and Sailors Memorial Arch in Hartford, Connecticut, and the James A. Garfield Memorial in Cleveland, Ohio. |
| Jul 10 | Paul Aloysius Hines (b. March 1, 1855) - National Association and Major League Baseball center fielder who was the first of only three players to achieve the batting Triple Crown in the 19th century. |
| Jul 17 | Cudjoe Kazoola Lewis (b. Oluale Kossola, circa 1841) - The third to last adult survivor of the Atlantic slave trade between Africa and the United States. |
| Jul 22 | William Mulholland (b. September 11, 1855) - Irish-American self-taught civil engineer who designed and supervised the building of the 233-mile-long Los Angeles Aqueduct. |
| Aug 1 | Arthur Dehon Little (b. December 15, 1863) - Chemist and chemical engineer who founded the consulting company Arthur D. Little. |
| Aug 14 | Harriet Mabel Spalding (b. January 10, 1862) - Litterateur and poet. |

August 15: William Penn Adair Rogers (b. November 4, 1879) - Vaudeville performer, actor and humorous social commentator. Born as a citizen of the Cherokee Nation, he traveled around the world three times, made 71 films, and wrote more than 4,000 nationally syndicated newspaper columns.

Rogers was hugely popular in the United States for his leading political wit and was the highest paid Hollywood film star of 1934. He died with aviator Wiley Post when their small airplane crashed in northern Alaska. *Photo: Will Rogers, circa 1933.*

| | |
|---|---|
| Aug 15 | Wiley Hardeman Post (b. November 22, 1898) - Aviator who was the first pilot to fly solo around the world. Post was posthumously inducted into the National Aviation Hall of Fame in 1969. |
| Aug 17 | Charlotte Perkins Gilman (b. July 3, 1860) - Humanist, feminist, novelist, writer, lecturer, eugenicist and advocate for social reform. Gilman was inducted into the National Women's Hall of Fame in 1994. |
| Aug 25 | Mack Swain (b. February 16, 1876) - Movie actor who appeared in many of Mack Sennett's comedies at Keystone Studios. Swain was honored with a star on the Hollywood Walk of Fame in 1960. |

| | |
|---|---|
| Aug 27 | Frederick Childe Hassam (b. October 17, 1859) - Impressionist painter, noted for his urban and coastal scenes, who produced over 3,000 paintings, oils, watercolors, etchings and lithographs over the course of his career. |
| Sep 8 | Edward Laurence Doheny (b. August 10, 1856) - Oil tycoon and philanthropist who in 1892 drilled the first successful oil well in the Los Angeles City Oil Field. |
| Sep 8 | Carl Austin Weiss Sr. (b. December 6, 1906) - Physician who assassinated Senator Huey Long. |
| Sep 10 | Huey Pierce Long Jr. (b. August 30, 1893) - Democratic Party politician who served as the 40th Governor of Louisiana (1928-1932), and as a Senator for Louisiana (1932-1935). |
| Sep 10 | Simeon Selby Pennewill (b. July 23, 1867) - Republican Party politician who served as the 53rd Governor of Delaware (1909-1913). |
| Sep 11 | Charles Norris (b. December 4, 1867) - New York's first appointed chief medical examiner (1918-1935), and pioneer of forensic toxicology in America. |
| Sep 18 | Alice Dunbar Nelson (b. July 19, 1875) - Poet, journalist and political activist who was among the first generation of African Americans born free in the Southern United States after the end of the American Civil War. |
| Sep 23 | William DeWolf Hopper (b. March 30, 1858) - Actor, singer, comedian and theatrical producer best known for performing the popular baseball poem "Casey at the Bat." |
| Sep 26 | Andy Adams (b. May 3, 1859) - Writer of western fiction. |
| Oct 7 | Francis Wilson (b. February 7, 1854) - Actor and founding president of the Actors' Equity Association. |
| Oct 12 | Loretta C. Van Hook (b. July 4, 1852) - Missionary and educator in Persia. |
| Oct 20 | Adolphus Washington Greely, FRSGS (b. March 27, 1844) - U.S. Army officer and leader of the eponymous polar expedition that got trapped in the wilderness for over three years. |
| Oct 23 | Charles Henry Buckius Demuth (b. November 8, 1883) - Precisionist painter. |
| Oct 24 | Dutch Schultz (b. Arthur Simon Flegenheimer; August 6, 1901) - New York City mobster. |
| Nov 6 | Henry Fairfield Osborn, Sr., FRS (b. August 8, 1857) - Paleontologist, geologist and eugenics advocate who was the president of the American Museum of Natural History for 25 years, and a co-founder of the American Eugenics Society. |
| Nov 6 | William Ashley Sunday (b. November 19, 1862) - Major League Baseball outfielder who was widely considered the most influential American evangelist during the first two decades of the 20th century. |
| Nov 17 | Ballard MacDonald (b. October 15, 1882) - Lyricist known for songs such as "The Trail of the Lonesome Pine" and "(Back Home Again in) Indiana." |
| Dec 2 | James Henry Breasted (b. August 27, 1865) - Archaeologist, Egyptologist and historian. |
| Dec 2 | Martha Carey Thomas (b. January 2, 1857) - Educator, suffragist and linguist. |
| Dec 14 | Stanley Grauman Weinbaum (b. April 4, 1902) - Science fiction writer. |
| Dec 16 | Thelma Alice Todd (b. July 29, 1906) - Actress and businesswoman who appeared in around 120 feature films and shorts (1926-1935). |
| Dec 28 | Clarence Shepard Day Jr. (b. November 18, 1874) - Author and cartoonist best known for his 1935 work "Life with Father." |

# POPULAR MUSIC

| | | |
|---|---|---|
| Fred Astaire | No.1 | Cheek To Cheek |
| Shirley Temple | No.2 | On The Good Ship Lollipop |
| Ray Noble & His Orchestra | No.3 | Isle Of Capri |
| Eddy Duchin & His Orchestra | No.4 | Lovely To Look At |
| Bing Crosby | No.5 | Red Sails In The Sunset |
| Fats Waller | No.6 | Truckin' |
| The Carter Family | No.7 | Can The Circle Be Unbroken |
| Glen Gray & His Orchestra | No.8 | Blue Moon |
| The Dorsey Brothers' Orchestra | No.9 | Lullaby Of Broadway |
| The Boswell Sisters | No.10 | The Object Of My Affection |

*NB: During this era music was dominated by a number of Big Bands and songs could be attributed to the band leader, the band name, the lead singer, or a combination of these. On top of this the success of a song was tied to the sales of sheet music, so a popular song would often be perfomed by many different combinations of singers and bands and the contemporary charts would list the song without clarifying whose version was the major hit. With this in mind although the above chart has been compiled with best intent it does remain subjective.*

**Fred Astaire
Cheek To Cheek**

| Label: | Written by: | Length: |
|---|---|---|
| Brunswick | Irving Berlin | 3 mins 18 secs |

**Fred Astaire** (b. May 10, 1899 - d. June 22, 1987) was a dancer, choreographer, singer, musician and actor who is widely regarded as the "greatest popular-music dancer of all time." During a career spanning some 76 years he received numerous accolades including an Honorary Academy Award in 1949. The song "Cheek to Cheek" featured in the movie Top Hat (1935), and was inducted into the Grammy Hall of Fame in 2000.

**Shirley Temple
On The Good Ship Lollipop**

| Label: | Written by: | Length: |
|---|---|---|
| His Master's Voice | Whiting / Clare | 3 mins 16 secs |

**Shirley Temple** (b. April 23, 1928 - d. February 10, 2014) was an actress, singer, dancer, and diplomat who was Hollywood's No.1 box-office draw from 1934 through 1938, and the first child actor to receive an Academy Award (1935). Temple first sang "On the Good Ship Lollipop" in the movie Bright Eyes (1934), and it became her signature song.

## Ray Noble & His Orchestra
## Isle Of Capri

| Label: | Written by: | Length: |
|--------|-------------|---------|
| Victor | Grosz / Kennedy | 3 mins 19 secs |

**Raymond Stanley Noble** (b. December 17, 1903 - d. April 2, 1978) was a jazz and big band musician who was a bandleader, composer and arranger, as well as a radio host, television and film comedian, and actor. Noble was inducted into the Big Band and Jazz Hall of Fame in 1987, and the Songwriters Hall of Fame in 1996.

---

## Eddy Duchin & His Orchestra
## Lovely To Look At

| Label: | Written by: | Length: |
|--------|-------------|---------|
| Victor | Fields / Kern / McHugh / Hammerstein II | 3 mins 1 sec |

**Edwin Frank Duchin** (b. April 1, 1909 - d. February 9, 1951) was a jazz pianist and bandleader during the 1930s and 1940s, and was famous for his engaging onstage personality and his elegant piano style. "Lovely to Look At" featured in the film Roberta (1935), and was nominated for the Academy Award for Best Song.

## ⑤ Bing Crosby
## Red Sails In The Sunset

| Label: | Written by: | Length: |
|---|---|---|
| Decca | Hugh Williams | 3 mins 13 secs |

**Harry Lillis Crosby, Jr.** (b. May 3, 1903 - d. October 14, 1977) was a singer and actor who was a leader in record sales, radio ratings, and motion picture grosses from 1931 through 1954. Crosby's trademark warm bass-baritone voice made him the best-selling recording artist of the 20$^{th}$ century, selling close to a billion records, tapes, compact discs and digital downloads worldwide. Other popular versions of "Red Sails in the Sunset" in 1935 were sung by Guy Lombardo, Mantovani, Jack Jackson, and Al Bowlly.

---

## ⑥ Fats Waller
## Truckin'

| Label: | Written by: | Length: |
|---|---|---|
| Victor | Bloom / Koehler | 3 mins 20 secs |

**Thomas Wright Waller** (b. May 21, 1904 - d. December 15, 1943) was a jazz pianist, organist, composer, singer, and comedic entertainer who was one of the most popular performers of his era. Waller achieved critical and commercial success across the United States and Europe, and his innovations to the Harlem stride style laid the groundwork for modern jazz piano.

## ⑦ The Carter Family
## Can The Circle Be Unbroken

| Label: | Written by: | Length: |
|--------|-------------|---------|
| Conqueror | Habershon / Gabriel | 3 mins 7 secs |

**The Carter Family** were a traditional folk music group that recorded between 1927 and 1956. Nicknamed "The First Family of Country Music," they had a profound influence on bluegrass, country, Southern gospel, pop and rock music. They were elected to the Country Music Hall of Fame in 1970, the Grammy Hall of Fame in 1988, and the International Bluegrass Music Hall of Honor in 2001.

---

## ⑧ Glen Gray & His Orchestra
## Blue Moon

| Label: | Written by: | Length: |
|--------|-------------|---------|
| Decca | Rodgers / Hart | 3 mins 14 secs |

**Glenn Gray Knoblauch** (b. June 7, 1900 - d. August 23, 1963), known professionally as Glen Gray, was a jazz saxophonist and leader of the Casa Loma Orchestra. Active from 1929 through 1947, and 1957 through 1963, the Casa Loma Orchestra was one of the top dance bands in North America.

# The Dorsey Brothers' Orchestra
# Lullaby Of Broadway

| Label: | Written by: | Length: |
|---|---|---|
| Decca | Warren / Dubin | 2 mins 44 secs |

**The Dorsey Brothers Orchestra** were a studio dance band led by Tommy Dorsey (b. November 19, 1905 - d. November 26, 1956) and Jimmy Dorsey (b. February 29, 1904 - d. June 12, 1957). The band was active from 1928 until 1935, when Tommy Dorsey permanently left the orchestra to take over the Joe Haymes band.

---

# The Boswell Sisters
# The Object Of My Affection

| Label: | Written by: | Length: |
|---|---|---|
| Columbia | Poe / Grier / Tomlin | 3 mins 20 secs |

**The Boswell Sisters** were a close harmony singing trio of the jazz and swing eras consisting of three sisters: Martha (b. June 9, 1905 - d. July 2, 1958), Connie (b. December 3, 1907 - d. October 11, 1976), and Helvetia (b. May 20, 1911 - d. November 12, 1988). The group split in 1936, but Connie continued on as a solo vocalist in radio, film and television for another 25 years.

# 1935: TOP MOVIES

1. **Mutiny on the Bounty** - *Metro-Goldwyn-Mayer*
2. **Top Hat** - *RKO Pictures*
3. **Broadway Melody of 1936** - *Metro-Goldwyn-Mayer*
4. **David Copperfield** - *Metro-Goldwyn-Mayer*
5. **The Bride of Frankenstein** - *Universal Pictures*

# OSCARS

**Best Picture:** Mutiny on the Bounty
**Most Nominations:** Mutiny on the Bounty (8)
**Most Wins:** The Informer (4)

*Victor McLaglen (with Louis B. Mayer and Clark Gable) / Bette Davis.*

The 8th Academy Awards, honoring the best in film for 1935, were presented on March 5, 1936, at the Biltmore Hotel in Los Angeles, California.

**Best Director:** John Ford - *The Informer*

**Best Actor:** Victor McLaglen - *The Informer*
**Best Actress:** Bette Davis – *Dangerous*

**Academy Honorary Award:** D. W. Griffith - "For his distinguished creative achievements as director and producer and his invaluable initiative and lasting contributions to the progress of the motion picture arts".

Directed by: Frank Lloyd - Runtime: 2h 12m

Fletcher Christian, the first mate of the HMS Bounty, leads a mutiny which results in his sadistic commander's unceremonious removal from the ship.

# Starring

**Charles Laughton**
*b. July 1, 1899*
*d. December 15, 1962*
**Character:**
Captain Bligh

**Clark Gable**
*b. February 1, 1901*
*d. November 16, 1960*
**Character:**
Fletcher Christian

**Franchot Tone**
*b. February 27, 1905*
*d. September 18, 1968*
**Character:**
Roger Byam

# Trivia

**Goof** | When Dr. Bacchus is telling to Christian how he lost his leg, the Bounty rolls, knocking him down, but the brandy bottle clearly remains on the table. In the next shot the bottle has disappeared.

**Interesting Facts** | Clark Gable initially felt he was badly miscast as an English naval lieutenant in the film, however, he later said that he thought it was the best movie he had ever starred in.

"Mutiny on the Bounty" is the only movie to receive three nominations for the Academy Award for Best Actor: Clark Gable, Charles Laughton, and Franchot Tone. They all lost to Victor McLaglen in The Informer (1935). *NB: The Academy introduced a Best Supporting Actor Oscar shortly afterward to ensure this situation would not be repeated.*

Wallace Beery turned down the role of Capt. Bligh because he didn't like Clark Gable and didn't want to be stuck on a long location shoot with him.

"Mutiny on the Bounty" was the last winner of an Oscar for Best Picture that didn't win any other Academy Awards. The only other movies that have done this are: The Broadway Melody (1929), and Grand Hotel (1932).

**Quote** | *Captain William Bligh:* What's your name?
*Seaman Thomas Ellison:* Thomas Ellison, sir. Pressed into service. I've got a wife, a baby!
*Captain William Bligh:* I asked your name, not the history of your misfortunes.

# TOP HAT

Directed by: Mark Sandrich - Runtime: 1h 41m

Dancer Jerry Travers, working for his good friend and producer Horace Hardwick, falls for model Dale Tremont. Complications arise when Dale mistakes Jerry for Horace.

# Starring

**Fred Astaire**
*b. May 10, 1899*
*d. June 22, 1987*
**Character:**
Jerry Travers

**Ginger Rogers**
*b. July 16, 1911*
*d. April 25, 1995*
**Character:**
Dale Tremont

**Edward Everett Horton**
*b. March 18, 1886*
*d. September 29, 1970*
**Character:**
Horace Hardwick

# Trivia

**Interesting Facts**

During the finale of the "Top Hat, White Tie and Tails" production number, perfectionist Fred Astaire was continually breaking his canes in frustration at his mistakes. Thirteen canes were prepared for the scene which, as it turns out, was successfully completed using the last intact cane.

Erik Rhodes's Italian characterization so offended the Italian government, and dictator Benito Mussolini in particular, that "Top Hat" was banned in Italy. The same fate had befallen The Gay Divorcee (1934) the year before.

Fred Astaire and Ginger Rogers dance together five times in this movie, the most times of any of their ten pictures together.

The Venice canal set was so large it required two adjoining sound stages at RKO's Gower studio. The entire length was over 300 feet which, up to that time, was the largest set ever built on the RKO lot.

The dress Ginger Rogers wears in "The Piccolino" number is on display in the Smithsonian's National Museum of American History in Washington, DC.

**Quotes**

*Dale Tremont:* How could I have ever fallen in love with a man like you!
[Dale slaps Jerry, then storms off]
*Jerry Travers:* She loves me.

*Jerry Travers:* In dealing with a girl or horse, one just lets nature take its course.

# BROADWAY MELODY OF 1936

Directed by: Roy Del Ruth / W.S. Van Dyke - Runtime: 1h 41m

A Broadway producer is reluctant to hire his high school sweetheart for the leading role in a new show, so she decides to take advantage of a rumor started by a gossip columnist.

# Starring

**Jack Benny**
*b. February 14, 1894*
*d. December 26, 1974*
**Character:**
Bert Keeler

**Eleanor Powell**
*b. November 21, 1912*
*d. February 11, 1982*
**Character:**
Irene Foster

**Robert Taylor**
*b. August 5, 1911*
*d. June 8, 1969*
**Character:**
Bob Gordon

# Trivia

**Goof** | During the "breakfast on the roof" scene, clothes appear and disappear between shots on the clothes line behind Ted (Buddy Ebsen).

**Interesting Facts** | Eleanor Powell reportedly did not want to be in the movie as she was slated for the non-dancing role eventually played by Una Merkel. Too much of a neophyte to confront studio executives, she tried to engineer her dismissal by politely demanding the lead role and an exorbitant salary. To her amazement the studio met her terms paving the way for her meteoric film career.

Buddy Ebsen, whose career spanned seven decades, made his debut in this movie.

Robert Wildhack does a humorous stint in the movie showcasing different snores. He is billed as "The Snorer." In the next movie in the series, Broadway Melody of 1938 (1937), he does sneezes, and is billed as "The Sneezer."

The radio announcer who introduces Bert Keeler (Jack Benny) is Don Wilson, the announcer on Benny's real-life radio program.

The singing voice of Eleanor Powell was dubbed by Marjorie Lane.

**Quote** | *Bert Keeler:* He wants to get in Gordon's show.
*Snoop:* Yeah, what do you do?
*The Snorer:* I snore.
*Snoop:* Oh, you're part of the audience.

# DAVID COPPERFIELD

W.C. FIELDS
FREDDIE·BARTHOLOMEW
LIONEL·BARRYMORE
MADGE·EVANS
MAUREEN·O'SULLIVAN
EDNA·MAY·OLIVER
LEWIS·STONE
FRANK·LAWTON
ELIZABETH·ALLAN
ROLAND·YOUNG

CHARLES DICKENS'
DAVID
COPPERFIELD
REGI: GEORGE CUKOR

Directed by: George Cukor - Runtime: 1h 47m

The adventures of David Copperfield on his journey from an unhappy and impoverished childhood through to adulthood.

# Starring

**W.C. Fields**
*b. January 29, 1880*
*d. December 25, 1946*
**Character:**
Micawber

**Freddie Bartholomew**
*b. March 28, 1924*
*d. January 23, 1992*
**Character:**
David (boy)

**Lionel Barrymore**
*b. April 28, 1878*
*d. November 15, 1954*
**Character:**
Dan Peggotty

# Trivia

**Interesting Facts**

According to film historians, this is the only picture in which W.C. Fields performs exactly according to script and as directed. Fields admired the Charles Dickens novel and wanted desperately to play Micawber, so he agreed to forgo his usual ad-libs and put aside his distaste at working with child actors.

Largely as a result of the box office success of this movie and Captains Courageous (1937), by the late 1930s, Freddie Bartholomew, who was discovered after an extensive casting search across both the U.S. and the U.K., was one of Hollywood's highest-paid child actors.

Several major characters were omitted from the original Dickens novel to keep the running time of this movie to under two hours, including Copperfield's close friend Thomas Traddles.

Two Charles Dickens movie adaptations were released in 1935, both produced by David O. Selznick, this movie and "A Tale of Two Cities". Both received Academy Award nominations for Best Picture.

**Quote**

*David Copperfield:* But why must I go away, Aunt Betsey? I want to stay with you, and Mr. Dick.
*Aunt Betsey:* But you have to be educated, David, and take your place in the world. There isn't a finer school in Canterbury than Dr. Strong's. You must make us proud, David. Never be mean in anything. Never be false. Never be cruel. Avoid these three vices, and I can always be hopeful of you.

# THE BRIDE OF FRANKENSTEIN

Directed by: James Whale - Runtime: 1h 15m

Baron Henry Frankenstein, goaded by the mad scientist Dr. Pretorius, creates a new creature, a woman, to be the companion of his monster.

# Starring

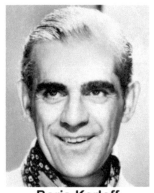

**Boris Karloff**
*b. November 23, 1887*
*d. February 2, 1969*
**Character:**
The Monster

**Elsa Lanchester**
*b. October 28, 1902*
*d. December 26, 1986*
**Character:**
The Monster's Bride

**Colin Clive**
*b. January 20, 1900*
*d. June 25, 1937*
**Character:**
Henry Frankenstein

# Trivia

**Goofs**

When Elizabeth is talking to Henry on the telephone, you can see her hand slip out of the ropes that have her tied up, then slip back inside the ropes again.

When Karl and the monster are climbing onto the parapet, the background can clearly be seen through their figures.

**Interesting Facts**

Colin Clive's alcoholism had worsened since his appearance in Frankenstein (1931), but James Whale did not recast the role because he believed Clive's "hysterical quality" was necessary for the movie.

Elsa Lanchester was only 5'4" but for the role was placed on stilts that made her 7' tall. The bandages were placed so tightly on her that she was unable to move and had to be carried about the studio and fed through a straw.

Marilyn Harris, who played Maria, the girl The Monster accidentally kills in the original Frankenstein movie, appears uncredited as another young girl. Director James Whale deliberately gave her a one-word line ("Look!"), so she would be paid more by the studio as an actor with a speaking role instead of as an extra.

Elsa Lanchester said that her spitting / hissing performance was inspired by the swans at Regent's Park in London. "They're really very nasty creatures" she said.

**Quotes**

*Doctor Pretorius:* To a new world of gods and monsters!

*The Monster:* [speaking to Frankenstein and Elizabeth] Go, you live.
*The Monster:* [turning to Doctor Pretorius] You stay, we belong dead.

# SPORTING WINNERS

## AP Associated Press

## MALE ATHLETE OF THE YEAR

# JOE LOUIS - BOXING

**Weight:** Heavyweight / **Height:** 6ft 1½in / **Reach:** 76in

**Joseph Louis Barrow** (b. May 13, 1914 - d. April 12, 1981) was a professional boxer who competed from 1934 to 1951. Nicknamed "the Brown Bomber," Louis is widely regarded as one of the greatest and most influential boxers of all time. He reigned as the world heavyweight champion from 1937 until his temporary retirement in 1949, and was victorious in 25 consecutive title defenses, a record for all weight classes. *Fun fact: Louis had the longest single reign as champion of any boxer in history.*

**Professional boxing record:**

| 69 Fights | 66 Wins | 3 Losses |
|---|---|---|
| By knockout | 52 | 2 |
| By decision | 13 | 1 |
| By disqualification | 1 | 0 |

Louis was named fighter of the year four times by The Ring magazine (1936, 1938, 1939, and 1941), and in 2005 was ranked as the best heavyweight of all time by the International Boxing Research Organization, and No.1 on The Ring magazine's list of the "100 greatest punchers of all time." Louis was inducted into the Boxing Hall of Fame in 1990.

**Associated Press**

## FEMALE ATHLETE OF THE YEAR

# HELEN WILLS MOODY - TENNIS

**Helen Newington Wills** (b. October 6, 1905 - d. January 1, 1998), also known by her married names Helen Wills Moody and Helen Wills Roark, was a World No.1 ranked tennis player who was the first American woman athlete to become a global celebrity. During her career she won 31 Grand Slam tournament titles, including 19 singles titles. She also won two gold medals at the 1924 Olympics in Paris, and was a member of the U.S. Wightman Cup team which won the cup 6 times (1923, 1927, 1929, 1931, 1932 and 1938).

**Grand Slam titles:**

| | | |
|---|---|---|
| French Open | Singles | 1928, 1929, 1930, 1932 |
| | Doubles | 1930, 1932 |
| Wimbledon | Singles | 1927, 1928, 1929, 1930, 1932, 1933, 1935, 1938 |
| | Doubles | 1924, 1927, 1930 |
| | Mixed doubles | 1929 |
| U.S. Open | Singles | 1923, 1924, 1925, 1927, 1928, 1929, 1931 |
| | Doubles | 1922, 1924, 1925, 1928 |
| | Mixed doubles | 1924, 1928 |

From 1919 through 1938, Wills amassed a 398-35 (91.9%) W/L match record, and had a 180-match win streak from 1927 until 1933. She was inducted into the International Tennis Hall of Fame in 1959, and the Women's Hall of Fame of the Intercollegiate Tennis Association in 1996. *NB: Jack Kramer, Harry Hopman, Mercer Beasley, Don Budge, and AP News called Wills the greatest female player in history and, in her obituary, The New York Times described her as "arguably the most dominant tennis player of the 20th century."*

# GOLF

## THE MASTERS - GENE SARAZEN

The Masters Tournament is the first of the majors to be played each year and unlike the other major championships it is played at the same location - Augusta National Golf Club, Georgia. This was the second ever Masters (officially known as the "Augusta National Invitation Tournament" for its first five editions) and was held April 4-8, 1935. Gene Sarazen beat runner up Craig Wood by five strokes after firing in a double eagle on the 15th hole of the final round to force a playoff. The total prize fund was $5,000 of which Sarazen took home $1,500.

## U.S. OPEN - SAM PARKS, JR.

The 39th edition of the U.S. Open Championship (established in 1895) was held June 6-8 at Oakmont Country Club in Oakmont, Pennsylvania, a suburb northeast of Pittsburgh. Sam Parks, Jr., a 25-year-old with no prior tournament wins, prevailed by two strokes in difficult scoring conditions to win his only major title. The total prize fund was $5,000 of which Parks took home $1,000.

## PGA CHAMPIONSHIP - JOHNNY REVOLTA

The 18th PGA Championship was held October 17-23 at Twin Hills Golf & Country Club in Oklahoma City, Oklahoma. Then a match play championship, Johnny Revolta won his only major title defeating Tommy Armour 5 & 4. The total prize fund was $7,820 of which Revolta took home $1,000.

Sam Parks, Jr.          Gene Sarazen          Johnny Revolta

# WORLD SERIES

**Detroit Tigers**

4 - 2

**Chicago Cubs**

Total attendance: 286,672 - Average attendance: 47,779
Winning player's share: $6,545 - Losing player's share: $4,199

The 1935 and 32nd World Series matched the Detroit Tigers against the Chicago Cubs - the Tigers won in six games for their first championship in five Series appearances (they had previously lost in 1907, 1908, 1909, and 1934).

|   | Date | Score | | | Location | Time | Att. |
|---|------|-------|---|---|----------|------|------|
| 1 | Oct 2 | **Chicago Cubs** | 3-0 | Detroit Tigers | Navin Field | 1:51 | 47,391 |
| 2 | Oct 3 | Chicago Cubs | 3-8 | **Detroit Tigers** | Navin Field | 1:59 | 46,742 |
| 3 | Oct 4 | **Detroit Tigers** | 6-5 | Chicago Cubs | Wrigley Field | 2:27 | 45,532 |
| 4 | Oct 5 | **Detroit Tigers** | 2-1 | Chicago Cubs | Wrigley Field | 2:28 | 49,350 |
| 5 | Oct 6 | Detroit Tigers | 1-3 | **Chicago Cubs** | Wrigley Field | 1:49 | 49,237 |
| 6 | Oct 7 | Chicago Cubs | 3-4 | **Detroit Tigers** | Navin Field | 1:57 | 48,420 |

# MLB SEASON SUMMARY

| Pos. | American League | W | L | PCT | GB | Home | Road |
|------|-----------------|---|---|-----|----|----|------|
| 1st | **Detroit Tigers** | **93** | **58** | **0.616** | - | **53-25** | **40-33** |
| 2nd | New York Yankees | 89 | 60 | 0.597 | 3 | 41-33 | 48-27 |
| 3rd | Cleveland Indians | 82 | 71 | 0.536 | 12 | 48-29 | 34-42 |
| 4th | Boston Red Sox | 78 | 75 | 0.510 | 16 | 41-37 | 37-38 |

American League MVP: Hank Greenberg - Detroit Tigers

| Pos. | National League | W | L | PCT | GB | Home | Road |
|------|-----------------|---|---|-----|----|----|------|
| 1st | **Chicago Cubs** | **100** | **54** | **0.649** | - | **56-21** | **44-33** |
| 2nd | St. Louis Cardinals | 96 | 58 | 0.623 | 4 | 53-24 | 43-34 |
| 3rd | New York Giants | 91 | 62 | 0.595 | 8½ | 50-27 | 41-35 |
| 4th | Pittsburgh Pirates | 86 | 67 | 0.562 | 13½ | 46-31 | 40-36 |

National League MVP: Gabby Hartnett - Chicago Cubs

# Horse Racing

**Omaha** (b. March 24, 1932 - d. April 24, 1959) was a champion American Thoroughbred racehorse who was the third winner of the Triple Crown. In a racing career which lasted from 1934 to 1936, Omaha won 9 of his 22 races. He had his greatest success as a three-year-old in 1935 when he swept the Triple Crown, winning the Kentucky Derby, Preakness Stakes and Belmont Stakes. *Photo: Omaha after winning the 1935 Belmont Stakes.*

## Kentucky Derby - Omaha

The Kentucky Derby is held annually on the first Saturday in May at Churchill Downs in Louisville, Kentucky, and is open to three-year-old thoroughbreds. It is a Grade 1 stakes race and is run over a distance of 10 furlongs (1¼ mile).

## Preakness Stakes - Omaha

The Preakness Stakes is held on the third Saturday in May each year at Pimlico Race Course in Baltimore, Maryland, and is open to three-year-old thoroughbreds. It is a Grade 1 stakes race run over a distance of 9½ furlongs (1³⁄₁₆ mile).

## Belmont Stakes - Omaha

The Belmont Stakes is held every June (on a Saturday between June 5 and 11) at Belmont Park in Elmont, New York, and is open to three-year-old thoroughbreds. It is a Grade 1 stakes race run over a distance of 12 furlongs (1½ mile).

# NFL CHAMPIONSHIP GAME

**New York Giants**  7 - 26  **Detroit Lions**

Played: December 15, 1935, at University of Detroit Stadium, Detroit, Michigan
Winning player's share: $313 - Losing player's share: $200
Attendance: 15,000 / Referee: Tommy Hughitt

## NFL SEASON SUMMARY

The 1935 NFL season was the 16th regular season of the National Football League. It concluded with the NFL Championship Game which saw the Detroit Lions defeat the to New York Giants 26-7.

### Eastern Division

| Team | P | W | L | T | PCT | DIV | PF | PA |
|---|---|---|---|---|---|---|---|---|
| **New York Giants** | **12** | **9** | **3** | **0** | **.750** | **8-0** | **180** | **96** |
| Brooklyn Dodgers | 12 | 5 | 6 | 1 | .455 | 3-4-1 | 90 | 141 |
| Pittsburgh Pirates | 12 | 4 | 8 | 0 | .333 | 3-5 | 100 | 209 |
| Boston Redskins | 11 | 2 | 8 | 1 | .200 | 2-4-1 | 65 | 123 |
| Philadelphia Eagles | 11 | 2 | 9 | 0 | .182 | 2-5 | 60 | 179 |

### Western Division

| Team | P | W | L | T | PCT | DIV | PF | PA |
|---|---|---|---|---|---|---|---|---|
| **Detroit Lions** | **12** | **7** | **3** | **2** | **.700** | **3-2-2** | **191** | **111** |
| Green Bay Packers | 12 | 8 | 4 | 0 | .667 | 4-4 | 181 | 96 |
| Chicago Cardinals | 12 | 6 | 4 | 2 | .600 | 3-2-2 | 99 | 97 |
| Chicago Bears | 12 | 6 | 4 | 2 | .600 | 1-3-2 | 192 | 106 |

Note: The NFL did not officially count tie games in the standings until 1972.

### League Leaders

| Passing | Rushing | Receiving | Touchdowns |
|---|---|---|---|
| Ed Danowski | Doug Russell | Charley Malone | Don Hutson |
| New York Giants | Chicago Cardinals | Boston Redskins | Green Bay Packers |
| 794 yards | 499 yards | 433 yards | 7 |

# STANLEY CUP

| Montreal Maroons | 3 - 0 | Toronto Maple Leafs |
|---|---|---|

|  | Date | Team | Result | Team | Stadium |
|---|---|---|---|---|---|
| 1 | Apr 4 | **Montreal Maroons** | 3-2 | Toronto Maple Leafs | Maple Leaf Gardens |
| 2 | Apr 6 | **Montreal Maroons** | 3-1 | Toronto Maple Leafs | Maple Leaf Gardens |
| 3 | Apr 9 | Toronto Maple Leafs | 1-4 | **Montreal Maroons** | Montreal Forum |

# NHL SEASON SUMMARY

The 1934-35 NHL season was the 18th season of the National Hockey League and featured 9 teams each playing 48 games. The season ended when the Montreal Maroons swept the Toronto Maple Leafs in three games in the Stanley Cup Finals.

### American Division

| Pos. | Team | GP | W | L | T | GF | GA | Diff | Pts |
|---|---|---|---|---|---|---|---|---|---|
| **1st** | **Boston Bruins** | **48** | **26** | **16** | **6** | **129** | **112** | **+17** | **58** |
| 2nd | Chicago Black Hawks | 48 | 26 | 17 | 5 | 118 | 88 | +30 | 57 |
| 3rd | New York Rangers | 48 | 22 | 20 | 6 | 137 | 139 | -2 | 50 |

### Canadian Division

| Pos. | Team | GP | W | L | T | GF | GA | Diff | Pts |
|---|---|---|---|---|---|---|---|---|---|
| **1st** | **Toronto Maple Leafs** | **48** | **30** | **14** | **4** | **157** | **111** | **+46** | **64** |
| 2nd | Montreal Maroons | 48 | 24 | 19 | 5 | 123 | 92 | +31 | 53 |
| 3rd | Montreal Canadiens | 48 | 19 | 23 | 6 | 110 | 145 | -35 | 44 |

### Scoring Leaders

|  | Player | Team | GP | Goals | Assists | Points | PIM |
|---|---|---|---|---|---|---|---|
| 1 | **Charlie Conacher** | **Toronto Maple Leafs** | **47** | **36** | **21** | **57** | **24** |
| 2 | Syd Howe | Eagles / Red Wings | 50 | 22 | 25 | 47 | 34 |
| 3 | Larry Aurie | Detroit Red Wings | 48 | 17 | 29 | 46 | 24 |
| 4 | Frank Boucher | New York Rangers | 48 | 13 | 32 | 45 | 2 |

Hart Trophy (Most Valuable Player): Eddie Shore - Boston Bruins
Vezina Trophy (Fewest Goals Allowed): Lorne Chabot - Chicago Black Hawks

# Boston Marathon

The Boston Marathon is the oldest annual marathon in the world and dates back to 1897.

**Race Result:**

| | | | |
|---|---|---|---|
| **1st** | **John Kelley** | **USA** | **2h:32m:07s** |
| 2nd | Pat Dengis | USA | 2h:34m:11s |
| 3rd | Richard Wilding | Canada | 2h:39m:50s |

# Indianapolis 500

The 23rd International 500-Mile Sweepstakes Race was held at the Indianapolis Motor Speedway on Thursday, May 30, 1935. The race was won by Kelly Petillo in front of a crowd of approximately 157,000 spectators; Wilbur Shaw came second and Bill Cummings came third. *Photo: Indy 500 winner Kelly Petillo (and his riding mechanic Jimmy Dunham) in the race winning Gilmore Speedway Special.*

# TENNIS - NATIONAL CHAMPIONSHIPS

**Men's Singles Champion - Wilmer Allison - United States**
**Ladies Singles Champion - Helen Jacobs - United States**

The 1935 U.S. National Championships (now known as the U.S. Open) took place on the outdoor grass courts at the West Side Tennis Club, Forest Hills in New York City, and ran from August 29 until September 12. It was the 55th staging of the U.S. National Championships and the fourth Grand Slam tennis event of 1935. *Photos: U.S. National Championships winners Helen Jacobs and Wilmer Allison.*

### Men's Singles Final

| Country | Player | Set 1 | Set 2 | Set 3 |
|---|---|---|---|---|
| United States | Wilmer Allison | 6 | 6 | 6 |
| United States | Sidney Wood | 2 | 2 | 3 |

### Women's Singles Final

| Country | Player | Set 1 | Set 2 |
|---|---|---|---|
| United States | Helen Jacobs | 6 | 6 |
| United States | Sarah Palfrey Cooke | 2 | 4 |

### Men's Doubles Final

| Country | Players | Set 1 | Set 2 | Set 3 | Set 4 | Set 5 |
|---|---|---|---|---|---|---|
| United States | Wilmer Allison / John Van Ryn | 6 | 6 | 2 | 3 | 6 |
| United States | Don Budge / Gene Mako | 2 | 3 | 6 | 6 | 1 |

### Women's Doubles Final

| Country | Players | Set 1 | Set 2 |
|---|---|---|---|
| United States | Helen Jacobs / Sarah Palfrey Cooke | 6 | 6 |
| United States | Carolin Babcock / Dorothy Andrus | 4 | 2 |

### Mixed Doubles Final

| Country | Players | Set 1 | Set 2 | Set 3 |
|---|---|---|---|---|
| United States / Spain | Sarah Palfrey Cooke / Enrique Maier | 6 | 4 | 6 |
| U.K. / Czechoslovakia | Kay Stammers / Roderich Menzel | 4 | 6 | 3 |

## Comparison Chart

| | 1935 | 1935 + Inflation | 2024 | % Change |
|---|---|---|---|---|
| House | $8,500 | $193,783 | $387,600 | +100.0% |
| Annual Income | $1000 | $22,798 | $72,228 | +216.8% |
| Car | $1,290 | $29,409 | $47,936 | +63.0% |
| Gallon of Gasoline | 14¢ | $3.19 | $3.27 | +2.5% |
| Gallon of Milk | 17¢ | $3.88 | $3.99 | +2.8% |
| New York Times | 2¢ | 46¢ | $4 | +769.6% |

# Groceries

|  |  |
|---|---|
| Bread (16oz loaf) | 6¢ |
| Wisconsin Cheese (per lb) | 25¢ |
| Pure Lard (per lb) | 15¢ |
| Peanut Butter (pint jar) | 17¢ |
| Ann Page Preserves (16oz jar) | 19¢ |
| Graham Crackers (2lb) | 23¢ |
| Grandmother's Round Layer Cake | 25¢ |
| Fig Bars (1lb) | 10¢ |
| Verigood Flour (48lb bag) | $1.65 |
| Snow White Pure Cane Sugar (10lb bag) | 53¢ |
| Granulated Sugar (10lb bag) | 50¢ |
| White House Milk (small cans) | 3¢ |
| Fine Table Salt (3x 1½lb) | 10¢ |
| Post Bran Flakes (2 pkgs.) | 19¢ |
| Seven Flavors Chewing Gum (4 pkgs.) | 10¢ |
| Apples (4lbs) | 25¢ |
| Oranges (12) | 21¢ |
| Lemons (12) | 20¢ |
| Golden Ripe Bananas (2 dozen) | 25¢ |
| Seedless Grapes (2lb) | 15¢ |
| Idaho Potatoes (10lb) | 19¢ |
| Green Head Cabbage (per lb) | 2¢ |
| A&P Fresh Tomatoes (2lb) | 15¢ |
| Roast Beef (per lb) | 11¢ |
| Stew Meat (per lb) | 7¢ |
| Veal Cutlets (per lb) | 23¢ |
| Cured Sliced Ham (per lb) | 29¢ |
| Decker's Sliced Bacon (per lb) | 35¢ |
| Dry Salt Jowls (per lb) | 21¢ |
| Lamb Chops (per lb) | 20¢ |
| Full Dressed Chicken Fryers (per lb) | 29¢ |
| Libby's Potted Meat (6 cans) | 19¢ |
| A&P Pink Salmon (1lb can) | 10¢ |
| Sardines (3 tall cans) | 25¢ |
| Mayfield Corn (3x #2 cans) | 25¢ |
| Del Monte Spinach (2x #2½ can) | 25¢ |
| Iona Salad Dressing (quart) | 27¢ |
| Del Monte Sliced Pineapple (2x #2 cans) | 33¢ |
| Eight O'Clock Coffee (per lb) | 15¢ |
| Liptons Tea (¼lb can) | 20¢ |
| Tender Leaf Tea (3½oz) | 17¢ |
| Coca Cola (bottle) | 5¢ |
| Del Monte Tomato Juice (3 cans) | 15¢ |
| Waldorf Tissue (4 rolls) | 15¢ |
| Palmolive Soap (3 bars) | 13¢ |
| Lux Laundry Soap | 22¢ |
| Vigo Dog Food (3 cans) | 16¢ |

# CASH STORES
## JACKSONS

## Bananas
Nice Size **ea 1c**

### ENGLISH
## Walnuts
Medium Size, lb............ **19c**

### Good POTATOES
**10 lbs 21c**

| | | |
|---|---|---|
| Cranberries | lb | 19c |
| Tangerines | Good Size, Dozen..... | 19c |
| Grapefruit | 2 for | 5c |
| Syrup | gallon | 39c |
| White Raisins | lb | 15c |
| Pop Corn | 2 lbs | 19c |

## Shortening 4 pound Carton... **55c**

### Groceries
| | | |
|---|---|---|
| Sugar | 10 lbs | 49c |
| Post-Bran | pkg | 10c |
| Flour | 24 pound Sack..... | 93c |
| Peaches | No. 2½ Can...... | 14c |
| Dog Food | Red Hart, 3 for | 25c |

### Coffee
CHASE & SANBORNS DATED
**lb 24c**

## Scott Tissue 2 ROLLS **15c**

### Bread
WHOLE WHEAT or WHITE
**ea 4½c**

### Bakery
| | | | |
|---|---|---|---|
| Fruit Cakes | Extra High Grade, | 2 lbs | 97c |
| Do-Nuts | | Doz | 15c |
| Sweet Rolls | | ea | 1c |
| ASSORTED LAYER Cakes ea | | | 17c |

## Fruit Cake Mix Complete Ingredients, Mixed **lb 37c**

| | | | |
|---|---|---|---|
| Sausage | Pure Pork | lb | 19c |
| Steak | Baby Beef | lb | 10c |
| Ground Meat | | lb | 12½c |
| Roast | Lean Pork | lb | 22c |
| Oysters | Selects, Pints | | 25c |
| Pork Steak | | lb | 25c |

### FRESH
## Fish
**lb 10c**

### DRESSED HENS
**lb 23c**

69

# Clothes

### Women's Clothing

| | |
|---|---|
| J.M. Dyer Fur Trimmed Coat | $23.75 |
| Brooks Winter Coat | $14.95 |
| Carter Fashion Shop Suit | $22.50 |
| Marks Bros. Suzette Frock | $1.98 |
| K. Wolens Spring Dress | $2.99 |
| Marks Bros. Blouse | from $1 |
| J.M. Dyer Satin Negligee | $5.95 |
| K. Wolens Silk Slip | 98¢ |
| J.M. Dyer Bloomers / Panties | $1 |
| Golden Art Hose | 79¢ |
| Austin Oxford Shoes | $4.95 |

### Men's Clothing

| | |
|---|---|
| Finis Farr Polo Topcoat | $15 |
| Harris & Jacobs Roamer Hat | $3.50 |
| Marks Bros. Tailored Griffon Suit | $25 |
| Marks Bros. Sweater | from $1.95 |
| Clermont Spring Shirt | $1.95 |
| Penney's Handmade Tie | 79¢ |
| J.M. Dyer Manhattan Pajamas | from $1.95 |
| Goldberg Leather Boots | $3.95 |
| Harris & Jacobs Interwoven Socks | 35¢ |

# Other Items

| | |
|---|---|
| Packard 120 Car | $980 |
| Ford V-8 Car | $510 |
| Chevrolet Master De Luxe Sport Sedan | $495 |
| Packard-Bell 5-Tube Car Radio | $25.95 |
| Western Auto 6V 13-Plate Battery | $2.65 |
| S.S. Columbia Bermuda Cruise (5½ days) | $65 |
| Hotel Charlotte Harbor - Florida (week) | $35 |
| Hotel Whitcomb - San Fransisco (per night) | $2 |
| Philco 7-Tube Radio | $54.95 |
| General Electric Sunlamp | $39.95 |
| Simmons Interspring Mattress | $19.95 |
| W. A. Rogers 29-Piece Silverware Service | $12.95 |
| 25-ft Garden Hose | $1.58 |
| Elgin 17-Jewel Pocket Watch | $75 |
| Elgin 15-Jewel Ladies Compact Watch | $39.75 |
| Streamline Ball Bearing Velocipede | $4.95 |
| All Steel Coaster Wagon | $2.95 |
| Streamline Electric Train | $5.95 |
| Monopoly Game | $2 |
| Side Valve Football | 95¢ |
| Kentucky Straight Whiskey (pint) | $1.07 |
| Angelica Port Sherry (quart) | 59¢ |
| Garcia Sublime Cigars (10) | 39¢ |
| Popular Brand Cigarettes | 15¢ |
| P.A. Tobacco (can) | 10¢ |
| Matches (3 boxes) | 10¢ |
| Snuff (6oz bottle) | 29¢ |

*1935* **CHEVROLET**

TURRET-TOP BODY BY FISHER (WITH FISHER VENTILATION SYSTEM) . . . IMPROVED
KNEE-ACTION RIDE . . . BLUE-FLAME VALVE-IN-HEAD ENGINE . . . WEATHER-
PROOF CABLE-CONTROLLED BRAKES . . . SHOCK-PROOF STEERING

*The Master De Luxe Sport Coupe*

**CHEVROLET**

# Money Conversion Table

| Amount | 1935 | 2024 |
|---|---|---|
| Penny | 1¢ | 23¢ |
| Nickel | 5¢ | $1.14 |
| Dime | 10¢ | $2.28 |
| Quarter Dollar | 25¢ | $5.70 |
| Half Dollar | 50¢ | $11.40 |
| Dollar | $1 | $22.80 |
| Two Dollars | $2 | $45.60 |
| Five Dollars | $5 | $113.99 |
| Ten Dollars | $10 | $227.98 |
| Twenty Dollars | $20 | $455.96 |
| Fifty Dollars | $50 | $1,139.90 |
| One Hundred Dollars | $100 | $2,279.80 |

Cumulative rate of inflation: 2179.8%

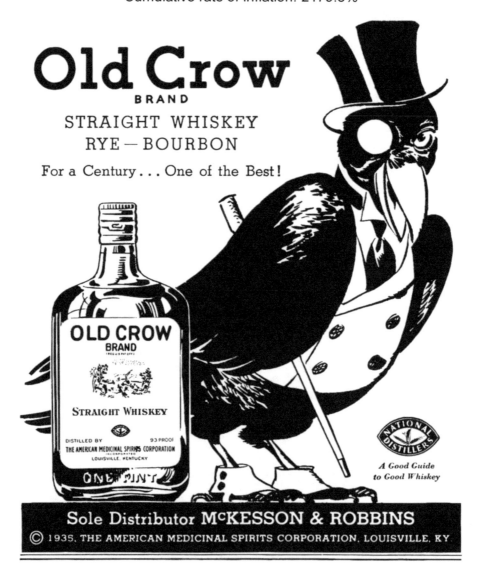

# U.S. Coins

| Official Circulated U.S. Coins | | Years Produced |
|---|---|---|
| Half-Cent | ½¢ | 1792 - 1857 |
| Cent (Penny) | 1¢ | 1793 - Present |
| 2-Cent | 2¢ | 1864 - 1873 |
| 3-Cent | 3¢ | 1851 - 1889 |
| Half-Dime | 5¢ | 1792 - 1873 |
| Five Cent Nickel | 5¢ | 1866 - Present |
| Dime | 10¢ | 1792 - Present |
| 20-Cent | 20¢ | 1875 - 1878 |
| Quarter | 25¢ | 1796 - Present |
| Half Dollar | 50¢ | 1794 - Present |
| Dollar Coin | $1 | 1794 - Present |
| Quarter Eagle | $2.50 | 1792 - 1929 |
| Three-Dollar Piece | $3 | 1854 - 1889 |
| Four-Dollar Piece | $4 | 1879 - 1880 |
| Half Eagle | $5 | 1795 – 1929 |
| Commemorative Half Eagle | $5 | 1980 - Present |
| Silver Eagle | $1 | 1986 - Present |
| Gold Eagle | $5 | 1986 - Present |
| Platinum Eagle | $10 - $100 | 1997 - Present |
| Double Eagle (Gold) | $20 | 1849 - 1933 |
| Half Union | $50 | 1915 |

Drink Coca-Cola
Delicious and Refreshing

COME AND GET IT

5¢

## Ice-cold every day in the year

Days are hot? Coca-Cola is cold, — ice-cold. Weather depressing?
Coca-Cola is refreshing, — so refreshing. Heat is everywhere; ice-
cold Coca-Cola is around the corner from anywhere. Why wait?

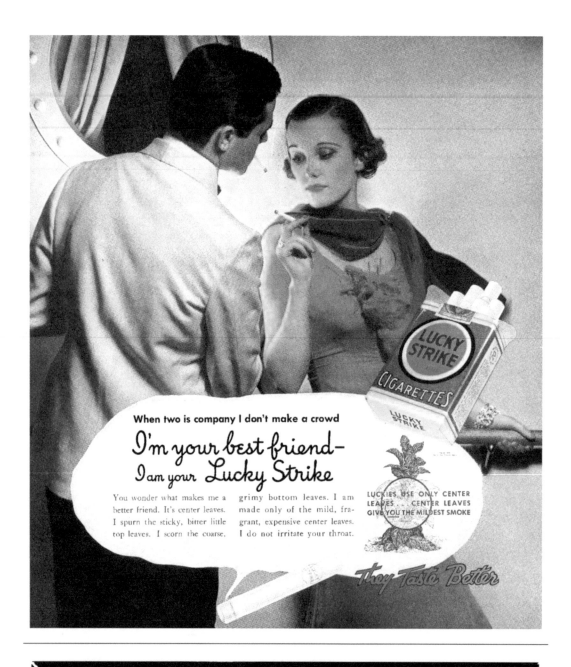

74

Made in United States
Cleveland, OH
06 December 2024